TODAY I AM GRATEFUL FOR

DEDICATION

This workbook is dedicated to everyone who has impacted my journey. I'm grateful for every soul because they've either been blessings or taught me lessons. Especially, thank you to my best friend, Alyssa, for introducing me to the spiritual world and starting my journey by gifting me my first Oracle Deck in high school. Thank you to my partner, Justin, for always endlessly encouraging me, believing in me, and for being such a bright light in my life. Thank you to my parents, Alice and Joe, for always supporting me, my art, my writing, and for giving me the confidence to go after my dreams. Thank you to the entire publishing team for making this workbook happen. And of course, thank you to you, the reader, for allowing me to be your guide on this journey. Sending you all so many blessings and so much love.

TODAY I AM GRATEFUL FOR

Erica Rose

chartwell
books

TABLE OF CONTENTS

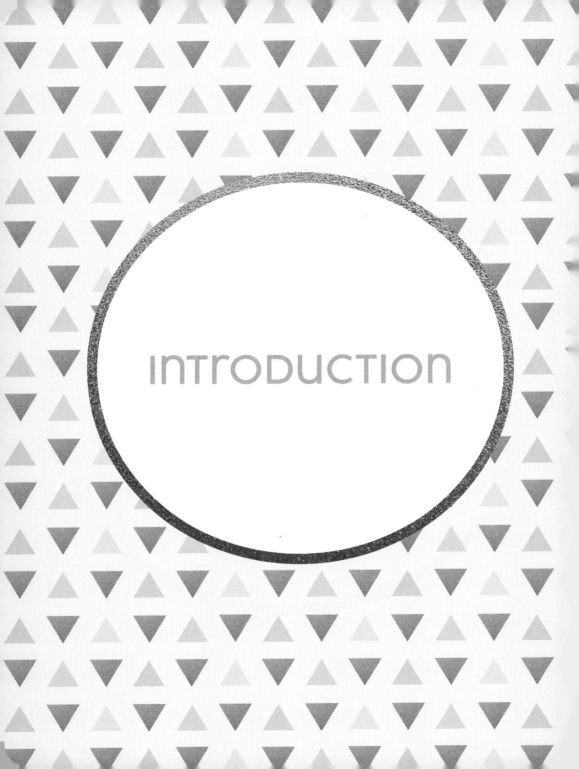

INTRODUCTION

If there's anything in this world that I want you to know, it's that you, beautiful soul, are absolutely amazing and that all the magic you need to make your dreams come true already exists inside you.

We live in an abundant universe with endless possibilities. Magic and miracles are all around us, constantly, every day. The universe is on your side. I promise you weren't sent here to continually be disappointed and fail. The universe wants to see you win and win big! You truly are a limitless being and anything is possible for you. No matter how large, scary, or unattainable your dreams may seem, you can make them happen.

Above all, I really want you to remember that your life purpose is your *life*. It's not to make a certain amount of money, it's not to collect a certain number of degrees and have the best job, it's not to get married and have a family by a certain age (or even at all), it's to just live. And most importantly, to live it the way you want to, not the way you think you're supposed to. Your purpose is to just be you, to follow what lights you up, and to enjoy the journey that is your life. You are not behind. You never were behind. There's no need to compare your journey to anyone else's because it's completely unique to you. You are a one-of-a-kind magical being sent here with the power to create your reality however you see fit. So long as you are staying true to yourself, being kind to all, and learning and growing, you absolutely are, without a doubt, headed in the right direction. If there's anything I've learned, it's that faith plus gratitude, combined with putting in the effort, absolutely can transform your life.

A few years ago, I was so tired of being in a job that made me overworked and miserable, having less than great finances, and a disappointing love life. I always had big dreams of a fabulous existence, one where I was doing spiritual work that excited me, where I was in the romantic relationship of my dreams, and felt secure financially. Above all, a life where I was happy. All evidence showed I was not living these dreams. Rather than sulking because everything was wrong, I actively chose to believe that one day it would all still happen. I started to switch my focus from what was wrong to what was right. Instead of thinking my finances weren't enough, I started to feel grateful for whatever money was coming in, knowing that more was on its way. I started creating oracle cards and doing spiritual work on the side, knowing that one day that would become my main career. I visualized meeting the most amazing partner and felt in my heart how it would feel to be so happy in love. I held the faith that my epic story was inevitable. The key to making your goals and dreams come true isn't waiting until you see to believe, it's to believe before you see.

A major action that really helped me maintain my faith and transform my mindset was journaling. Journaling daily and writing empowering affirmations really helps bring clarity. This practice provides a safe space for you to explore what it is you really want out of life. It allows you to properly feel all of your emotions and to release everything that no longer serves you. Journaling gives you a moment to count your blessings and appreciate all that you already have.

I'm happy to say that by sticking to a regular journaling routine I am finally doing spiritual work as my main job (including my lifelong dream of being published—yay to this workbook!), am in a much better spot financially, and am in an amazing relationship.

I know that sometimes life can seem overwhelming. Sometimes we're just so anxious about everything that is wrong or everything that could go wrong, comparing, feeling behind or inadequate, regretting past mistakes, or worrying about the future so much that we forget to just live in the present. Our mindset is a major factor in manifesting our dreams. Living in the present and focusing on the good can change everything. Our brains often need to hear something many times before it'll start to truly accept and believe it. That's why it's so important to stick with these daily exercises, because the more you practice your affirmations, express gratitude, and imagine you are living your desired reality, the more your brain will start to accept it as your truth.

Once your mind accepts it as your truth, you'll naturally start to embody that energy, thus making you an energetic match to receive your fully manifested desires.

I've created this workbook to help you live in the moment, transform your mindset, manifest your goals, maintain the faith, and find joy in your journey. The formula I've designed within will help you stay on track and focused, so if you're ready for your personal metamorphosis, dedicate yourself to filling this workbook out daily.

Overall, just remember that it's easy to give up when things don't work immediately, but I promise you if you keep it up, keep doing this inner work, and keep refusing to subscribe to the reality you don't want, and instead keep fully believing in yourself and your dreams, it can all absolutely happen for you.

You got this and you can do this!

HOW TO USE THIS BOOK

In order to track our progress, we must first acknowledge where we already are. The beginning of this workbook has an initial assessment asking you to analyze where you're at in each area of your life, figure out where you'd like to be, and of course, appreciate everything you've already achieved.

Now you can get started with your daily work. At the start of each week, there is a thought-provoking prompt for you to write about. Every day will consist of easy, navigable tasks—such as writing affirmations, acknowledging your emotions, feeling gratitude, and visualizing your dreams. The daily and weekly prompts will both repeat, but repetition is vital in solidifying your new mindset.

The affirmations are presented in "I am" format because "I am" is the most powerful statement in the universe. Whatever you say after these words becomes your truth so, choose your words wisely. The universe doesn't accept negatives, so avoid saying phrases like "I am not" or "I am never." Focus on the good aspect. If you'd like to be stress-free, don't say, "I am stress-free" because the universe will still hear it as "I am stressed." Instead change it to, "I am peaceful. I am calm." Focusing on positive affirmations will make a huge impact.

Another major moment of transformation is understanding that it's so important to fully feel all your emotions. People often tend to shy away from the darker, sad, or mad emotions because they feel like it'll attract more negativity, but that's actually not true. If you push down those emotions and feign happiness on top of them, you never give them a chance to heal.

This workbook includes a mood tracker in order to give you a moment to acknowledge your feelings daily. It's perfectly okay and normal to have a mad or sad day; it doesn't mean you're on the wrong track, it means you're human. Embrace all of your emotions. Feel them, honor them, and then when you're ready, let them go. Choose to focus on the good and lift yourself up.

There's also space for you to track the phases of the moon. We organic beings are mostly made of water, so just as the moon affects the ocean tides, it's going to affect our inner tides. I encourage you to look up what phase the moon is in every day. Doing this may help you further predict your emotions. For example, imagine you come to realize there's a pattern that whenever it's a full moon, you're extra stressed. So now, going forward, once you know the full moon is coming, you can take time to be more gentle with yourself and take preventive measures to help yourself be less stressed.

Another major theme of this workbook is gratitude, as it really does transform lives. Each day it's important to take a look around and acknowledge just how many blessings you have. We often get so used to what we have that we tend to focus on what's missing and what we still have yet to achieve. An important change you can make is to start truly appreciating all the things you already have and all the things you've already achieved. The universe loves a grateful heart. When you acknowledge your blessings and genuinely feel grateful for everything you have, it opens you up to receive more. You become a magnet for even more blessings.

At the end of each week, I included a space for you to acknowledge something good that happened. When we choose to focus on the good things rather than the bad, it shifts our vibration and puts us in a better mindset to achieve happiness, gratitude, and manifest our goals.

Visualization is another powerful tool in your arsenal. Our subconscious plays a huge part in manifesting. In the way our words become our truth, our thoughts and visions become our truth as well. Your subconscious mind can't tell the difference between what's actually happening and what's being imagined, so it's great to use that in your favor. You don't need to focus on the how or when, just keep visualizing the what and the why. See what you want happening, acknowledge why you want it to happen, and above all, really *feel* it happening. Feel all the feelings of excitement and everything you'd feel if it actually happened. Seeing and feeling it puts that energy out into the universe and starts the manifestation process. I encourage you to visualize and really feel what you want to manifest for at least two to five minutes a day, and afterwards you can mark off the checkbox.

I've also included another checkbox to help you release what's no longer serving you. Just like honoring your emotions, I want you to take a moment to imagine everything that's bothering you surrounded in beautiful white light then dissolving away, signifying the situation is completely healed. Imagine that what's bothering you is solved, and feel how relieved you'd feel if it were so.

It's vital to take a daily moment of self-care. Even if it's just five minutes a day, doing something for yourself helps to reset your energy. Whether it's exercising, meditating, resting, watching a great show, or even eating your favorite meal, it's so important to fill up your cup by doing something each day that brings a smile to your face. When you've done that—you can mark off that checkbox as well!

This workbook will be your guide for an entire year. If you stick with this practice, you'll absolutely see improvement in your mindset as you rewire your brain to automatically focus on gratitude. Once you've completed the full year, there will be a final assessment which encourages you to analyze just how far you've come, what you've manifested, and how changing your mindset changed your life.

Now, go make your life magical!

MY INITIAL REFLECTION

The best place to begin your journey is by analyzing where you currently are in each area of your life. Doing this will help you gain clarity about your mindset and give you space to decide what you wish to experience. Take some time to think and fill out each square in the chart below.

	Describe what you're currently experiencing in this area.
Career/School	
Finances	
Romantic relationships	
Relationships with friends and family	
Health and wellness	
Self-esteem and self-love	
Fun, travel, free time, hobbies	

Describe what you wish to change.

Dig deep. What are some limiting beliefs you may have in this area? What about your mindset is holding you back?

Career/School

Finances

Romantic relationships

Relationships with friends and family

Health and wellness

Self-esteem and self-love

Fun, travel, free time, hobbies

Reframe these limiting beliefs and write an empowering affirmation for each area.

Write what you wish to experience in each area. Write in the present tense, as if it has already happened.

List ten things that you're proud of yourself for already achieving.

List ten things that you currently do like about your life.

In order of importance, what five things would you love to manifest within the next year?

Describe how you would feel if these manifested into your reality.

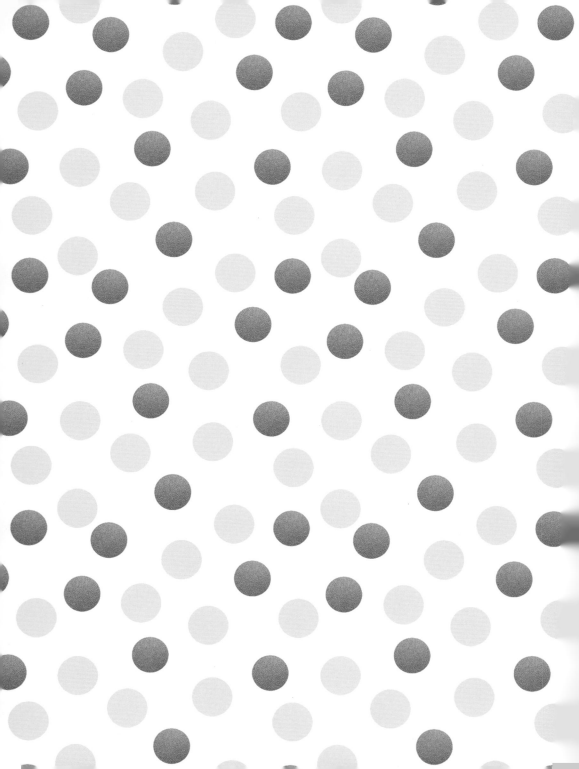

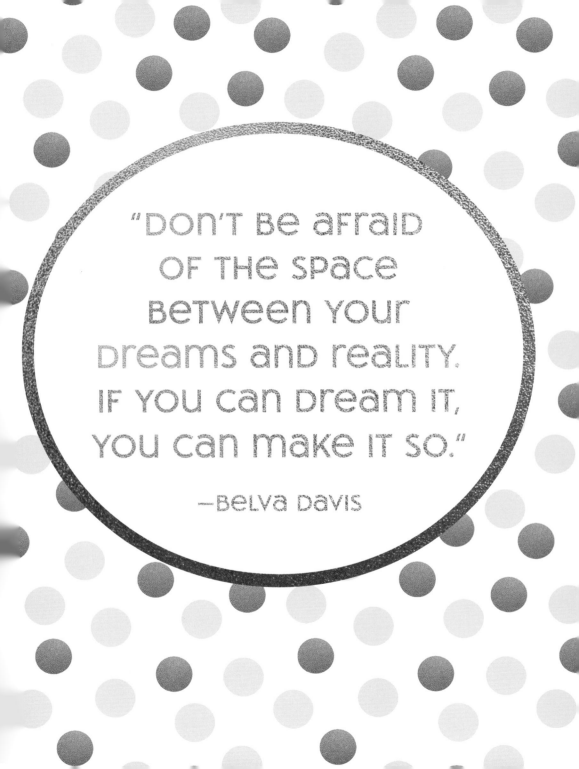

"DON'T BE AFRAID
OF THE SPACE
BETWEEN YOUR
DREAMS AND REALITY.
IF YOU CAN DREAM IT,
YOU CAN MAKE IT SO."

—BELVA DAVIS

What are the fears and worries you have about chasing your dreams?

week 1

If money were not an issue, you knew you couldn't fail, and all your dreams came true, what would your ideal life be like? Write in the present tense as if you are already living it! Get as detailed as possible to help you gain clarity. This is a great exercise to repeat because the more you write it out in present tense, the more it'll feel real to you and help you manifest it.

_____

_____

_____

MONDAY: _____ / _____   **MOOD:** _____   **MOON PHASE** ◯

My "I am" Affirmation of the day: _____

Today I am grateful for: _____

_____

I am manifesting: _____

☐ I visualized my dream coming true for 2-5 minutes.   ☐ I realized what no longer serves me & imagined my problems healed.   ☐ I made time for self-care today.

TUESDAY: _____ / _____   **MOOD:** _____   **MOON PHASE** ◯

My "I am" Affirmation of the day: _____

Today I am grateful for: _____

_____

I am manifesting: _____

☐ I visualized my dream coming true for 2-5 minutes.   ☐ I realized what no longer serves me & imagined my problems healed.   ☐ I made time for self-care today.

WEDNESDAY: _____ / _____   **MOOD:** _____   **MOON PHASE** ◯

My "I am" Affirmation of the day: _____

Today I am grateful for: _____

_____

I am manifesting: _____

☐ I visualized my dream coming true for 2-5 minutes.   ☐ I realized what no longer serves me & imagined my problems healed.   ☐ I made time for self-care today.

"The beginning is the most important part of the work." —Plato

THURSDAY: _____ / _____ **MOOD:** _____ **MOON PHASE** ○

My "I am" Affirmation of the day: _____

Today I am grateful for: _____

I am manifesting: _____

☐ I visualized my dream coming true for 2-5 minutes.   ☐ I realized what no longer serves me & imagined my problems healed.   ☐ I made time for self-care today.

FRIDAY: _____ / _____ **MOOD:** _____ **MOON PHASE** ○

My "I am" Affirmation of the day: _____

Today I am grateful for: _____

I am manifesting: _____

☐ I visualized my dream coming true for 2-5 minutes.   ☐ I realized what no longer serves me & imagined my problems healed.   ☐ I made time for self-care today.

SATURDAY: _____ / _____ **MOOD:** _____ **MOON PHASE** ○

My "I am" Affirmation of the day: _____

Today I am grateful for: _____

I am manifesting: _____

☐ I visualized my dream coming true for 2-5 minutes.   ☐ I realized what no longer serves me & imagined my problems healed.   ☐ I made time for self-care today.

SUNDAY: _____ / _____ **MOOD:** _____ **MOON PHASE** ○

My "I am" Affirmation of the day: _____

Today I am grateful for: _____

I am manifesting: _____

☐ I visualized my dream coming true for 2-5 minutes.   ☐ I realized what no longer serves me & imagined my problems healed.   ☐ I made time for self-care today.

THE BEST THING THAT HAPPENED TO ME THIS WEEK WAS:

week 2

It's always great to give yourself space to deeply heal and let go, so it's time to release everything that's bothering you. Write down anything that's currently bringing you down, no matter how small, and then imagine letting it all go. After that, write about the things that you love in your life. Focus on the things that make you smile and make your heart happy.

_____

_____

_____

MONDAY: _____ / _____   **MOOD:** _____   **MOON PHASE** ⚪

My "I am" Affirmation of the day: _____

Today I am grateful for: _____

I am manifesting: _____

☐ I visualized my dream coming true for 2–5 minutes.   ☐ I realized what no longer serves me & imagined my problems healed.   ☐ I made time for self-care today.

TUESDAY: _____ / _____   **MOOD:** _____   **MOON PHASE** ⚪

My "I am" Affirmation of the day: _____

Today I am grateful for: _____

I am manifesting: _____

☐ I visualized my dream coming true for 2–5 minutes.   ☐ I realized what no longer serves me & imagined my problems healed.   ☐ I made time for self-care today.

WEDNESDAY: _____ / _____   **MOOD:** _____   **MOON PHASE** ⚪

My "I am" Affirmation of the day: _____

Today I am grateful for: _____

I am manifesting: _____

☐ I visualized my dream coming true for 2–5 minutes.   ☐ I realized what no longer serves me & imagined my problems healed.   ☐ I made time for self-care today.

THURSDAY: _____ / _____   **MOOD:** _____   **MOON PHASE** ⚪

My "I am" Affirmation of the day: _____

Today I am grateful for: _____

_____

I am manifesting: _____

_____

☐ I visualized my dream coming true for 2-5 minutes.   ☐ I realized what no longer serves me & imagined my problems healed.   ☐ I made time for self-care today.

FRIDAY: _____ / _____   **MOOD:** _____   **MOON PHASE** ⚪

My "I am" Affirmation of the day: _____

Today I am grateful for: _____

_____

I am manifesting: _____

_____

☐ I visualized my dream coming true for 2-5 minutes.   ☐ I realized what no longer serves me & imagined my problems healed.   ☐ I made time for self-care today.

SATURDAY: _____ / _____   **MOOD:** _____   **MOON PHASE** ⚪

My "I am" Affirmation of the day: _____

Today I am grateful for: _____

_____

I am manifesting: _____

_____

☐ I visualized my dream coming true for 2-5 minutes.   ☐ I realized what no longer serves me & imagined my problems healed.   ☐ I made time for self-care today.

SUNDAY: _____ / _____   **MOOD:** _____   **MOON PHASE** ⚪

My "I am" Affirmation of the day: _____

Today I am grateful for: _____

_____

I am manifesting: _____

_____

☐ I visualized my dream coming true for 2-5 minutes.   ☐ I realized what no longer serves me & imagined my problems healed.   ☐ I made time for self-care today.

THE BEST THING THAT HAPPENED TO ME THIS WEEK WAS:

week 3

A fairy godmother is granting you three wishes. What would they be? She's also letting you grant one wish to everyone you love. What would they be? After each, take a moment to really envision it happening for yourself and the others.

_____

_____

_____

MONDAY: _____ / _____   **MOOD:** _____   **MOON PHASE** ◯

My "I am" Affirmation of the day: _____

Today I am grateful for: _____

I am manifesting: _____

☐ I visualized my dream coming true for 2-5 minutes.   ☐ I realized what no longer serves me & imagined my problems healed.   ☐ I made time for self-care today.

TUESDAY: _____ / _____   **MOOD:** _____   **MOON PHASE** ◯

My "I am" Affirmation of the day: _____

Today I am grateful for: _____

I am manifesting: _____

☐ I visualized my dream coming true for 2-5 minutes.   ☐ I realized what no longer serves me & imagined my problems healed.   ☐ I made time for self-care today.

WEDNESDAY: _____ / _____   **MOOD:** _____   **MOON PHASE** ◯

My "I am" Affirmation of the day: _____

Today I am grateful for: _____

I am manifesting: _____

☐ I visualized my dream coming true for 2-5 minutes.   ☐ I realized what no longer serves me & imagined my problems healed.   ☐ I made time for self-care today.

"Happiness will never come to those who fail to appreciate what they already have." —Buddha

THURSDAY: _____ / _____   **MOOD:** _____   **MOON PHASE** ○

My "I am" Affirmation of the day: _____

Today I am grateful for: _____

_____

I am manifesting: _____

☐ I visualized my dream coming true for 2-5 minutes.   ☐ I realized what no longer serves me & imagined my problems healed.   ☐ I made time for self-care today.

FRIDAY: _____ / _____   **MOOD:** _____   **MOON PHASE** ○

My "I am" Affirmation of the day: _____

Today I am grateful for: _____

_____

I am manifesting: _____

☐ I visualized my dream coming true for 2-5 minutes.   ☐ I realized what no longer serves me & imagined my problems healed.   ☐ I made time for self-care today.

SATURDAY: _____ / _____   **MOOD:** _____   **MOON PHASE** ○

My "I am" Affirmation of the day: _____

Today I am grateful for: _____

_____

I am manifesting: _____

☐ I visualized my dream coming true for 2-5 minutes.   ☐ I realized what no longer serves me & imagined my problems healed.   ☐ I made time for self-care today.

SUNDAY: _____ / _____   **MOOD:** _____   **MOON PHASE** ○

My "I am" Affirmation of the day: _____

Today I am grateful for: _____

_____

I am manifesting: _____

☐ I visualized my dream coming true for 2-5 minutes.   ☐ I realized what no longer serves me & imagined my problems healed.   ☐ I made time for self-care today.

THE BEST THING THAT HAPPENED TO ME THIS WEEK WAS:

week 4

See the true beauty in yourself. Write what you appreciate about yourself—both your external appearance and your personality.

_____

_____

_____

MONDAY: _____ / _____   MOOD: _____   MOON PHASE ○

My "I am" Affirmation of the day: _____

Today I am grateful for: _____

I am manifesting: _____

| ☐ | I visualized my dream coming true for 2-5 minutes. | ☐ | I realized what no longer serves me & imagined my problems healed. | ☐ | I made time for self-care today. |

TUESDAY: _____ / _____   MOOD: _____   MOON PHASE ○

My "I am" Affirmation of the day: _____

Today I am grateful for: _____

I am manifesting: _____

| ☐ | I visualized my dream coming true for 2-5 minutes. | ☐ | I realized what no longer serves me & imagined my problems healed. | ☐ | I made time for self-care today. |

WEDNESDAY: _____ / _____   MOOD: _____   MOON PHASE ○

My "I am" Affirmation of the day: _____

Today I am grateful for: _____

I am manifesting: _____

| ☐ | I visualized my dream coming true for 2-5 minutes. | ☐ | I realized what no longer serves me & imagined my problems healed. | ☐ | I made time for self-care today. |

THURSDAY: _____ / _____ **MOOD:** _____ **MOON PHASE** ⚪

My "I am" Affirmation of the day: _____

Today I am grateful for: _____

I am manifesting: _____

☐ I visualized my dream coming true for 2-5 minutes.   ☐ I realized what no longer serves me & imagined my problems healed.   ☐ I made time for self-care today.

FRIDAY: _____ / _____ **MOOD:** _____ **MOON PHASE** ⚪

My "I am" Affirmation of the day: _____

Today I am grateful for: _____

I am manifesting: _____

☐ I visualized my dream coming true for 2-5 minutes.   ☐ I realized what no longer serves me & imagined my problems healed.   ☐ I made time for self-care today.

SATURDAY: _____ / _____ **MOOD:** _____ **MOON PHASE** ⚪

My "I am" Affirmation of the day: _____

Today I am grateful for: _____

I am manifesting: _____

☐ I visualized my dream coming true for 2-5 minutes.   ☐ I realized what no longer serves me & imagined my problems healed.   ☐ I made time for self-care today.

SUNDAY: _____ / _____ **MOOD:** _____ **MOON PHASE** ⚪

My "I am" Affirmation of the day: _____

Today I am grateful for: _____

I am manifesting: _____

☐ I visualized my dream coming true for 2-5 minutes.   ☐ I realized what no longer serves me & imagined my problems healed.   ☐ I made time for self-care today.

THE BEST THING THAT HAPPENED TO ME THIS WEEK WAS:

week 5

Your feelings construct your manifestations. Create some good feelings by writing about the happiest days of your life. As you write them down, take a moment to really feel all the emotions you felt those days. This will help you attract more amazing days and will cultivate gratitude for past experiences.

_____

_____

_____

MONDAY: ____ / ____   **MOOD:** _____   **MOON PHASE** ◯

My "I am" Affirmation of the day: _____

Today I am grateful for: _____

I am manifesting: _____

☐ I visualized my dream coming true for 2-5 minutes. ☐ I realized what no longer serves me & imagined my problems healed. ☐ I made time for self-care today.

TUESDAY: ____ / ____   **MOOD:** _____   **MOON PHASE** ◯

My "I am" Affirmation of the day: _____

Today I am grateful for: _____

I am manifesting: _____

☐ I visualized my dream coming true for 2-5 minutes. ☐ I realized what no longer serves me & imagined my problems healed. ☐ I made time for self-care today.

WEDNESDAY: ____ / ____   **MOOD:** _____   **MOON PHASE** ◯

My "I am" Affirmation of the day: _____

Today I am grateful for: _____

I am manifesting: _____

☐ I visualized my dream coming true for 2-5 minutes. ☐ I realized what no longer serves me & imagined my problems healed. ☐ I made time for self-care today.

"Life is change. Growth is optional. Choose wisely." —Author Unknown

THURSDAY: _____ / _____   **MOOD:** _____   **MOON PHASE** ◯

My "I am" Affirmation of the day: _____
Today I am grateful for: _____
_____

I am manifesting: _____
_____

☐ I visualized my dream coming true for 2-5 minutes.   ☐ I realized what no longer serves me & imagined my problems healed.   ☐ I made time for self-care today.

FRIDAY: _____ / _____   **MOOD:** _____   **MOON PHASE** ◯

My "I am" Affirmation of the day: _____
Today I am grateful for: _____
_____

I am manifesting: _____
_____

☐ I visualized my dream coming true for 2-5 minutes.   ☐ I realized what no longer serves me & imagined my problems healed.   ☐ I made time for self-care today.

SATURDAY: _____ / _____   **MOOD:** _____   **MOON PHASE** ◯

My "I am" Affirmation of the day: _____
Today I am grateful for: _____
_____

I am manifesting: _____
_____

☐ I visualized my dream coming true for 2-5 minutes.   ☐ I realized what no longer serves me & imagined my problems healed.   ☐ I made time for self-care today.

SUNDAY: _____ / _____   **MOOD:** _____   **MOON PHASE** ◯

My "I am" Affirmation of the day: _____
Today I am grateful for: _____
_____

I am manifesting: _____
_____

☐ I visualized my dream coming true for 2-5 minutes.   ☐ I realized what no longer serves me & imagined my problems healed.   ☐ I made time for self-care today.

THE BEST THING THAT HAPPENED TO ME THIS WEEK WAS:

week 6

Gratitude Spree: List everything you are grateful for. Start small with things like your fingertips, your bed, your eyesight, and build to larger things like your best friend and every cent you have in the bank.

_____

_____

_____

MONDAY: _____ / _____   **MOOD:** _____   **MOON PHASE** ◯

My "I am" Affirmation of the day: _____

Today I am grateful for: _____

I am manifesting: _____

☐ I visualized my dream coming true for 2-5 minutes.   ☐ I realized what no longer serves me & imagined my problems healed.   ☐ I made time for self-care today.

TUESDAY: _____ / _____   **MOOD:** _____   **MOON PHASE** ◯

My "I am" Affirmation of the day: _____

Today I am grateful for: _____

I am manifesting: _____

☐ I visualized my dream coming true for 2-5 minutes.   ☐ I realized what no longer serves me & imagined my problems healed.   ☐ I made time for self-care today.

WEDNESDAY: _____ / _____   **MOOD:** _____   **MOON PHASE** ◯

My "I am" Affirmation of the day: _____

Today I am grateful for: _____

I am manifesting: _____

☐ I visualized my dream coming true for 2-5 minutes.   ☐ I realized what no longer serves me & imagined my problems healed.   ☐ I made time for self-care today.

THURSDAY: _____ / _____   **MOOD:** _____   **MOON PHASE** ○

My "I am" Affirmation of the day: _____

Today I am grateful for: _____

I am manifesting: _____

☐ I visualized my dream coming true for 2-5 minutes.   ☐ I realized what no longer serves me & imagined my problems healed.   ☐ I made time for self-care today.

FRIDAY: _____ / _____   **MOOD:** _____   **MOON PHASE** ○

My "I am" Affirmation of the day: _____

Today I am grateful for: _____

I am manifesting: _____

☐ I visualized my dream coming true for 2-5 minutes.   ☐ I realized what no longer serves me & imagined my problems healed.   ☐ I made time for self-care today.

SATURDAY: _____ / _____   **MOOD:** _____   **MOON PHASE** ○

My "I am" Affirmation of the day: _____

Today I am grateful for: _____

I am manifesting: _____

☐ I visualized my dream coming true for 2-5 minutes.   ☐ I realized what no longer serves me & imagined my problems healed.   ☐ I made time for self-care today.

SUNDAY: _____ / _____   **MOOD:** _____   **MOON PHASE** ○

My "I am" Affirmation of the day: _____

Today I am grateful for: _____

I am manifesting: _____

☐ I visualized my dream coming true for 2-5 minutes.   ☐ I realized what no longer serves me & imagined my problems healed.   ☐ I made time for self-care today.

THE BEST THING THAT HAPPENED TO ME THIS WEEK WAS:

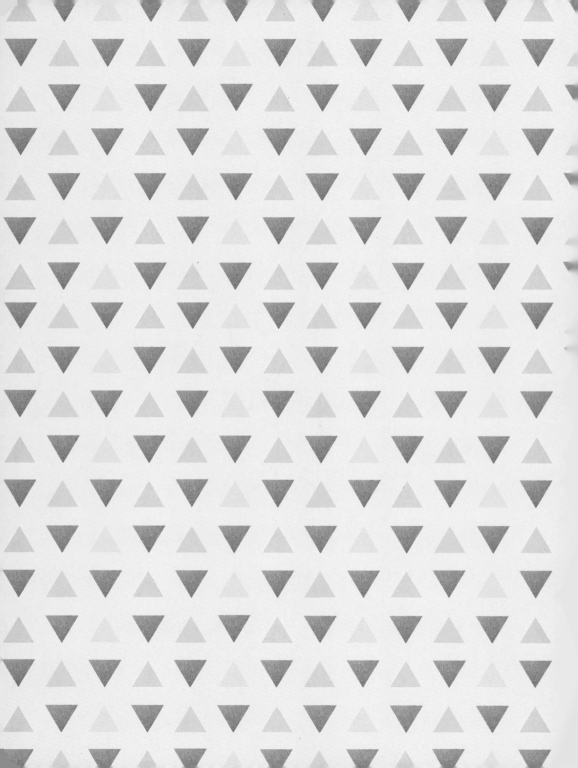

WHAT'S MEANT FOR
YOU WILL NEVER PASS YOU.
TRUST YOU ARE ALWAYS
BEING LED DOWN THE BEST
PATH POSSIBLE. IT WILL ALL
HAPPEN FOR YOU IN TRUE
DIVINE TIMING.

Write about a time where something didn't initially work out the way you wanted, but then later on you realized it was actually a blessing in disguise and you were led to something better. Was it with a job or relationship? This is proof that the universe always has your back.

week 7

If money were not an issue, you knew you couldn't fail, and all your dreams came true, what would your ideal life be like? Write in the present tense as if you are already living it. Get as detailed as possible to help you gain clarity.

_____

_____

_____

MONDAY: _____ / _____   MOOD: _____   MOON PHASE ◯

My "I am" Affirmation of the day: _____

Today I am grateful for: _____

I am manifesting: _____

☐ I visualized my dream coming true for 2-5 minutes.   ☐ I realized what no longer serves me & imagined my problems healed.   ☐ I made time for self-care today.

TUESDAY: _____ / _____   MOOD: _____   MOON PHASE ◯

My "I am" Affirmation of the day: _____

Today I am grateful for: _____

I am manifesting: _____

☐ I visualized my dream coming true for 2-5 minutes.   ☐ I realized what no longer serves me & imagined my problems healed.   ☐ I made time for self-care today.

WEDNESDAY: _____ / _____   MOOD: _____   MOON PHASE ◯

My "I am" Affirmation of the day: _____

Today I am grateful for: _____

I am manifesting: _____

☐ I visualized my dream coming true for 2-5 minutes.   ☐ I realized what no longer serves me & imagined my problems healed.   ☐ I made time for self-care today.

"When life takes away, something of greater value is always given in return." —Michael J. Fox

THURSDAY: _____ / _____   **MOOD:** _____   **MOON PHASE** ◯

My "I am" Affirmation of the day: _____

Today I am grateful for: _____

I am manifesting: _____

☐ I visualized my dream coming true for 2-5 minutes.   ☐ I realized what no longer serves me & imagined my problems healed.   ☐ I made time for self-care today.

FRIDAY: _____ / _____   **MOOD:** _____   **MOON PHASE** ◯

My "I am" Affirmation of the day: _____

Today I am grateful for: _____

I am manifesting: _____

☐ I visualized my dream coming true for 2-5 minutes.   ☐ I realized what no longer serves me & imagined my problems healed.   ☐ I made time for self-care today.

SATURDAY: _____ / _____   **MOOD:** _____   **MOON PHASE** ◯

My "I am" Affirmation of the day: _____

Today I am grateful for: _____

I am manifesting: _____

☐ I visualized my dream coming true for 2-5 minutes.   ☐ I realized what no longer serves me & imagined my problems healed.   ☐ I made time for self-care today.

SUNDAY: _____ / _____   **MOOD:** _____   **MOON PHASE** ◯

My "I am" Affirmation of the day: _____

Today I am grateful for: _____

I am manifesting: _____

☐ I visualized my dream coming true for 2-5 minutes.   ☐ I realized what no longer serves me & imagined my problems healed.   ☐ I made time for self-care today.

THE BEST THING THAT HAPPENED TO ME THIS WEEK WAS:

week 8

It's always great to give yourself space to deeply heal and let go, so it's time to release everything that's bothering you. Write down anything that's currently bringing you down, no matter how small, and then imagine letting it all go. After that, write about the things that you love in your life. Focus on the things that make you smile and make your heart happy.

_____

_____

_____

MONDAY: _____ / _____   **MOOD:** _____   **MOON PHASE** ⚪

My "I am" Affirmation of the day: _____

Today I am grateful for: _____

_____

I am manifesting: _____

☐ I visualized my dream coming true for 2–5 minutes. ☐ I realized what no longer serves me & imagined my problems healed. ☐ I made time for self-care today.

TUESDAY: _____ / _____   **MOOD:** _____   **MOON PHASE** ⚪

My "I am" Affirmation of the day: _____

Today I am grateful for: _____

_____

I am manifesting: _____

☐ I visualized my dream coming true for 2–5 minutes. ☐ I realized what no longer serves me & imagined my problems healed. ☐ I made time for self-care today.

WEDNESDAY: _____ / _____   **MOOD:** _____   **MOON PHASE** ⚪

My "I am" Affirmation of the day: _____

Today I am grateful for: _____

_____

I am manifesting: _____

☐ I visualized my dream coming true for 2–5 minutes. ☐ I realized what no longer serves me & imagined my problems healed. ☐ I made time for self-care today.

THURSDAY: _____ / _____   **MOOD:** _____   **MOON PHASE** ⚪

My "I am" Affirmation of the day: _____

Today I am grateful for: _____

I am manifesting: _____

☐ I visualized my dream coming true for 2-5 minutes.   ☐ I realized what no longer serves me & imagined my problems healed.   ☐ I made time for self-care today.

FRIDAY: _____ / _____   **MOOD:** _____   **MOON PHASE** ⚪

My "I am" Affirmation of the day: _____

Today I am grateful for: _____

I am manifesting: _____

☐ I visualized my dream coming true for 2-5 minutes.   ☐ I realized what no longer serves me & imagined my problems healed.   ☐ I made time for self-care today.

SATURDAY: _____ / _____   **MOOD:** _____   **MOON PHASE** ⚪

My "I am" Affirmation of the day: _____

Today I am grateful for: _____

I am manifesting: _____

☐ I visualized my dream coming true for 2-5 minutes.   ☐ I realized what no longer serves me & imagined my problems healed.   ☐ I made time for self-care today.

SUNDAY: _____ / _____   **MOOD:** _____   **MOON PHASE** ⚪

My "I am" Affirmation of the day: _____

Today I am grateful for: _____

I am manifesting: _____

☐ I visualized my dream coming true for 2-5 minutes.   ☐ I realized what no longer serves me & imagined my problems healed.   ☐ I made time for self-care today.

THE BEST THING THAT HAPPENED TO ME THIS WEEK WAS:

week 9

A fairy godmother is granting you three wishes. What would they be? She's also letting you grant one wish to everyone you love. What would they be? After each, take a moment to really envision it happening for yourself and the others.

_____

_____

_____

MONDAY: ____ / ____   **MOOD:** _____   **MOON PHASE** ◯

My "I am" Affirmation of the day: _____

Today I am grateful for: _____

I am manifesting: _____

☐ I visualized my dream coming true for 2-5 minutes.   ☐ I realized what no longer serves me & imagined my problems healed.   ☐ I made time for self-care today.

TUESDAY: ____ / ____   **MOOD:** _____   **MOON PHASE** ◯

My "I am" Affirmation of the day: _____

Today I am grateful for: _____

I am manifesting: _____

☐ I visualized my dream coming true for 2-5 minutes.   ☐ I realized what no longer serves me & imagined my problems healed.   ☐ I made time for self-care today.

WEDNESDAY: ____ / ____   **MOOD:** _____   **MOON PHASE** ◯

My "I am" Affirmation of the day: _____

Today I am grateful for: _____

I am manifesting: _____

☐ I visualized my dream coming true for 2-5 minutes.   ☐ I realized what no longer serves me & imagined my problems healed.   ☐ I made time for self-care today.

"Cherish your visions and your dreams as they are the children of your soul, the blueprints of your ultimate achievements." —Napoleon Hill

THURSDAY: _____ / _____   **MOOD:** _____   **MOON PHASE** ○

My "I am" Affirmation of the day: _____

Today I am grateful for: _____

I am manifesting: _____

☐ I visualized my dream coming true for 2-5 minutes.   ☐ I realized what no longer serves me & imagined my problems healed.   ☐ I made time for self-care today.

FRIDAY: _____ / _____   **MOOD:** _____   **MOON PHASE** ○

My "I am" Affirmation of the day: _____

Today I am grateful for: _____

I am manifesting: _____

☐ I visualized my dream coming true for 2-5 minutes.   ☐ I realized what no longer serves me & imagined my problems healed.   ☐ I made time for self-care today.

SATURDAY: _____ / _____   **MOOD:** _____   **MOON PHASE** ○

My "I am" Affirmation of the day: _____

Today I am grateful for: _____

I am manifesting: _____

☐ I visualized my dream coming true for 2-5 minutes.   ☐ I realized what no longer serves me & imagined my problems healed.   ☐ I made time for self-care today.

SUNDAY: _____ / _____   **MOOD:** _____   **MOON PHASE** ○

My "I am" Affirmation of the day: _____

Today I am grateful for: _____

I am manifesting: _____

☐ I visualized my dream coming true for 2-5 minutes.   ☐ I realized what no longer serves me & imagined my problems healed.   ☐ I made time for self-care today.

THE BEST THING THAT HAPPENED TO ME THIS WEEK WAS:

week 10

See the true beauty in yourself. Write what you appreciate about yourself—both your external appearance and your personality.

_____

_____

_____

MONDAY: _____ / _____   MOOD: _____   MOON PHASE ◯

My "I am" Affirmation of the day: _____

Today I am grateful for: _____

I am manifesting: _____

☐ I visualized my dream coming true for 2-5 minutes.　　☐ I realized what no longer serves me & imagined my problems healed.　　☐ I made time for self-care today.

TUESDAY: _____ / _____   MOOD: _____   MOON PHASE ◯

My "I am" Affirmation of the day: _____

Today I am grateful for: _____

I am manifesting: _____

☐ I visualized my dream coming true for 2-5 minutes.　　☐ I realized what no longer serves me & imagined my problems healed.　　☐ I made time for self-care today.

WEDNESDAY: _____ / _____   MOOD: _____   MOON PHASE ◯

My "I am" Affirmation of the day: _____

Today I am grateful for: _____

I am manifesting: _____

☐ I visualized my dream coming true for 2-5 minutes.　　☐ I realized what no longer serves me & imagined my problems healed.　　☐ I made time for self-care today.

THURSDAY: _____ / _____   **MOOD:** _____   **MOON PHASE** ◯

My "I am" Affirmation of the day: _____

Today I am grateful for: _____

I am manifesting: _____

☐ I visualized my dream coming true for 2-5 minutes.   ☐ I realized what no longer serves me & imagined my problems healed.   ☐ I made time for self-care today.

FRIDAY: _____ / _____   **MOOD:** _____   **MOON PHASE** ◯

My "I am" Affirmation of the day: _____

Today I am grateful for: _____

I am manifesting: _____

☐ I visualized my dream coming true for 2-5 minutes.   ☐ I realized what no longer serves me & imagined my problems healed.   ☐ I made time for self-care today.

SATURDAY: _____ / _____   **MOOD:** _____   **MOON PHASE** ◯

My "I am" Affirmation of the day: _____

Today I am grateful for: _____

I am manifesting: _____

☐ I visualized my dream coming true for 2-5 minutes.   ☐ I realized what no longer serves me & imagined my problems healed.   ☐ I made time for self-care today.

SUNDAY: _____ / _____   **MOOD:** _____   **MOON PHASE** ◯

My "I am" Affirmation of the day: _____

Today I am grateful for: _____

I am manifesting: _____

☐ I visualized my dream coming true for 2-5 minutes.   ☐ I realized what no longer serves me & imagined my problems healed.   ☐ I made time for self-care today.

THE BEST THING THAT HAPPENED TO ME THIS WEEK WAS:

week 11

Your feelings construct your manifestations. Create some good feelings by writing about the happiest days of your life. As you write them down, take a moment to really feel all the emotions you felt those days. This will help you attract more amazing days and will cultivate gratitude for past experiences.

_____

_____

_____

MONDAY: _____ / _____   MOOD: _____   MOON PHASE ○

My "I am" Affirmation of the day: _____

Today I am grateful for: _____

I am manifesting: _____

☐ I visualized my dream coming true for 2-5 minutes.   ☐ I realized what no longer serves me & imagined my problems healed.   ☐ I made time for self-care today.

TUESDAY: _____ / _____   MOOD: _____   MOON PHASE ○

My "I am" Affirmation of the day: _____

Today I am grateful for: _____

I am manifesting: _____

☐ I visualized my dream coming true for 2-5 minutes.   ☐ I realized what no longer serves me & imagined my problems healed.   ☐ I made time for self-care today.

WEDNESDAY: _____ / _____   MOOD: _____   MOON PHASE ○

My "I am" Affirmation of the day: _____

Today I am grateful for: _____

I am manifesting: _____

☐ I visualized my dream coming true for 2-5 minutes.   ☐ I realized what no longer serves me & imagined my problems healed.   ☐ I made time for self-care today.

"Some people want it to happen, some wish it would happen, others make it happen." —Michael Jordan

THURSDAY: _____ / _____   **MOOD:** _____   **MOON PHASE** ◯

My "I am" Affirmation of the day: _____

Today I am grateful for: _____

I am manifesting: _____

☐ I visualized my dream coming true for 2-5 minutes.   ☐ I realized what no longer serves me & imagined my problems healed.   ☐ I made time for self-care today.

FRIDAY: _____ / _____   **MOOD:** _____   **MOON PHASE** ◯

My "I am" Affirmation of the day: _____

Today I am grateful for: _____

I am manifesting: _____

☐ I visualized my dream coming true for 2-5 minutes.   ☐ I realized what no longer serves me & imagined my problems healed.   ☐ I made time for self-care today.

SATURDAY: _____ / _____   **MOOD:** _____   **MOON PHASE** ◯

My "I am" Affirmation of the day: _____

Today I am grateful for: _____

I am manifesting: _____

☐ I visualized my dream coming true for 2-5 minutes.   ☐ I realized what no longer serves me & imagined my problems healed.   ☐ I made time for self-care today.

SUNDAY: _____ / _____   **MOOD:** _____   **MOON PHASE** ◯

My "I am" Affirmation of the day: _____

Today I am grateful for: _____

I am manifesting: _____

☐ I visualized my dream coming true for 2-5 minutes.   ☐ I realized what no longer serves me & imagined my problems healed.   ☐ I made time for self-care today.

THE BEST THING THAT HAPPENED TO ME THIS WEEK WAS:

week 12

Gratitude Spree: List everything you are grateful for. Start small with things like your fingertips, your bed, your eyesight, and build to larger things like your best friend and every cent you have in the bank.

_____

_____

_____

MONDAY: ____ / ____   MOOD: _____   MOON PHASE ⚪

My "I am" Affirmation of the day: _____

Today I am grateful for: _____

I am manifesting: _____

☐ I visualized my dream coming true for 2-5 minutes. ☐ I realized what no longer serves me & imagined my problems healed. ☐ I made time for self-care today.

TUESDAY: ____ / ____   MOOD: _____   MOON PHASE ⚪

My "I am" Affirmation of the day: _____

Today I am grateful for: _____

I am manifesting: _____

☐ I visualized my dream coming true for 2-5 minutes. ☐ I realized what no longer serves me & imagined my problems healed. ☐ I made time for self-care today.

WEDNESDAY: ____ / ____   MOOD: _____   MOON PHASE ⚪

My "I am" Affirmation of the day: _____

Today I am grateful for: _____

I am manifesting: _____

☐ I visualized my dream coming true for 2-5 minutes. ☐ I realized what no longer serves me & imagined my problems healed. ☐ I made time for self-care today.

THURSDAY: _____ / _____   MOOD: _____   MOON PHASE ○

My "I am" Affirmation of the day: _____

Today I am grateful for: _____

_____

I am manifesting: _____

☐ I visualized my dream coming true for 2-5 minutes.   ☐ I realized what no longer serves me & imagined my problems healed.   ☐ I made time for self-care today.

FRIDAY: _____ / _____   MOOD: _____   MOON PHASE ○

My "I am" Affirmation of the day: _____

Today I am grateful for: _____

_____

I am manifesting: _____

☐ I visualized my dream coming true for 2-5 minutes.   ☐ I realized what no longer serves me & imagined my problems healed.   ☐ I made time for self-care today.

SATURDAY: _____ / _____   MOOD: _____   MOON PHASE ○

My "I am" Affirmation of the day: _____

Today I am grateful for: _____

_____

I am manifesting: _____

☐ I visualized my dream coming true for 2-5 minutes.   ☐ I realized what no longer serves me & imagined my problems healed.   ☐ I made time for self-care today.

SUNDAY: _____ / _____   MOOD: _____   MOON PHASE ○

My "I am" Affirmation of the day: _____

Today I am grateful for: _____

_____

I am manifesting: _____

☐ I visualized my dream coming true for 2-5 minutes.   ☐ I realized what no longer serves me & imagined my problems healed.   ☐ I made time for self-care today.

THE BEST THING THAT HAPPENED TO ME THIS WEEK WAS:

NO ONE IS
WORTHY OF DIMMING
YOUR LIGHT. YOU HAVE
ALL THE POWER SO
KEEP SHINING BRIGHT!

Close your eyes and imagine a beautiful ray of rainbow light coming down from the universe and into your crown chakra (located on the top of your head). Imagine that glowing rainbow light filling up your entire body, head to toe. Envision it surrounding you and encasing you in a beautiful bubble. You are now safe, you are now protected. No one's words or actions can truly bring you down while you are in your bubble of light. Use this practice as often as you'd like to ease anxiety, protect you from negative people, and to heal.

How do you feel after doing this exercise? What emotions did it bring up?

week 13

If money were not an issue, you knew you couldn't fail, and all your dreams came true, what would your ideal life be like? Write in the present tense as if you are already living it. Get as detailed as possible to help you gain clarity.

_____

_____

_____

MONDAY: _____ / _____   **MOOD:** _____   **MOON PHASE** ⬤

My "I am" Affirmation of the day: _____

Today I am grateful for: _____

I am manifesting: _____

☐ I visualized my dream coming true for 2-5 minutes.   ☐ I realized what no longer serves me & imagined my problems healed.   ☐ I made time for self-care today.

TUESDAY: _____ / _____   **MOOD:** _____   **MOON PHASE** ⬤

My "I am" Affirmation of the day: _____

Today I am grateful for: _____

I am manifesting: _____

☐ I visualized my dream coming true for 2-5 minutes.   ☐ I realized what no longer serves me & imagined my problems healed.   ☐ I made time for self-care today.

WEDNESDAY: _____ / _____   **MOOD:** _____   **MOON PHASE** ⬤

My "I am" Affirmation of the day: _____

Today I am grateful for: _____

I am manifesting: _____

☐ I visualized my dream coming true for 2-5 minutes.   ☐ I realized what no longer serves me & imagined my problems healed.   ☐ I made time for self-care today.

"With the new day comes new strength and new thoughts." —Eleanor Roosevelt

THURSDAY: ____ / ____   **MOOD:** _____   **MOON PHASE** ○

My "I am" Affirmation of the day: _____

Today I am grateful for: _____

_____

I am manifesting: _____

_____

☐ I visualized my dream coming true for 2-5 minutes.   ☐ I realized what no longer serves me & imagined my problems healed.   ☐ I made time for self-care today.

FRIDAY: ____ / ____   **MOOD:** _____   **MOON PHASE** ○

My "I am" Affirmation of the day: _____

Today I am grateful for: _____

_____

I am manifesting: _____

_____

☐ I visualized my dream coming true for 2-5 minutes.   ☐ I realized what no longer serves me & imagined my problems healed.   ☐ I made time for self-care today.

SATURDAY: ____ / ____   **MOOD:** _____   **MOON PHASE** ○

My "I am" Affirmation of the day: _____

Today I am grateful for: _____

_____

I am manifesting: _____

_____

☐ I visualized my dream coming true for 2-5 minutes.   ☐ I realized what no longer serves me & imagined my problems healed.   ☐ I made time for self-care today.

SUNDAY: ____ / ____   **MOOD:** _____   **MOON PHASE** ○

My "I am" Affirmation of the day: _____

Today I am grateful for: _____

_____

I am manifesting: _____

_____

☐ I visualized my dream coming true for 2-5 minutes.   ☐ I realized what no longer serves me & imagined my problems healed.   ☐ I made time for self-care today.

THE BEST THING THAT HAPPENED TO ME THIS WEEK WAS:

week 14

It's always great to give yourself space to deeply heal and let go, so it's time to release everything that's bothering you. Write down anything that's currently bringing you down, no matter how small, and then imagine letting it all go. After that, write about the things that you love in your life. Focus on the things that make you smile and make your heart happy.

_____

_____

_____

MONDAY: ____ / ____   **MOOD:** _____   **MOON PHASE** ⬤

My "I am" Affirmation of the day: _____

Today I am grateful for: _____

I am manifesting: _____

☐ I visualized my dream coming true for 2-5 minutes.   ☐ I realized what no longer serves me & imagined my problems healed.   ☐ I made time for self-care today.

TUESDAY: ____ / ____   **MOOD:** _____   **MOON PHASE** ⬤

My "I am" Affirmation of the day: _____

Today I am grateful for: _____

I am manifesting: _____

☐ I visualized my dream coming true for 2-5 minutes.   ☐ I realized what no longer serves me & imagined my problems healed.   ☐ I made time for self-care today.

WEDNESDAY: ____ / ____   **MOOD:** _____   **MOON PHASE** ⬤

My "I am" Affirmation of the day: _____

Today I am grateful for: _____

I am manifesting: _____

☐ I visualized my dream coming true for 2-5 minutes.   ☐ I realized what no longer serves me & imagined my problems healed.   ☐ I made time for self-care today.

THURSDAY: _____ / _____   MOOD: _____   MOON PHASE ⚪

My "I am" Affirmation of the day: _____
Today I am grateful for: _____
_____
I am manifesting: _____

☐ I visualized my dream   ☐ I realized what no longer serves me   ☐ I made time for
  coming true for 2-5 minutes.   & imagined my problems healed.   self-care today.

FRIDAY: _____ / _____   MOOD: _____   MOON PHASE ⚪

My "I am" Affirmation of the day: _____
Today I am grateful for: _____
_____
I am manifesting: _____

☐ I visualized my dream   ☐ I realized what no longer serves me   ☐ I made time for
  coming true for 2-5 minutes.   & imagined my problems healed.   self-care today.

SATURDAY: _____ / _____   MOOD: _____   MOON PHASE ⚪

My "I am" Affirmation of the day: _____
Today I am grateful for: _____
_____
I am manifesting: _____

☐ I visualized my dream   ☐ I realized what no longer serves me   ☐ I made time for
  coming true for 2-5 minutes.   & imagined my problems healed.   self-care today.

SUNDAY: _____ / _____   MOOD: _____   MOON PHASE ⚪

My "I am" Affirmation of the day: _____
Today I am grateful for: _____
_____
I am manifesting: _____

☐ I visualized my dream   ☐ I realized what no longer serves me   ☐ I made time for
  coming true for 2-5 minutes.   & imagined my problems healed.   self-care today.

THE BEST THING THAT HAPPENED TO ME THIS WEEK WAS:

week 15

A fairy godmother is granting you three wishes. What would they be? She's also letting you grant one wish to everyone you love. What would they be? After each, take a moment to really envision it happening for yourself and the others.

_____

_____

_____

MONDAY: _____/_____   **MOOD:** _____   **MOON PHASE** ◯

My "I am" Affirmation of the day: _____

Today I am grateful for: _____

I am manifesting: _____

☐ I visualized my dream coming true for 2–5 minutes. ☐ I realized what no longer serves me & imagined my problems healed. ☐ I made time for self-care today.

TUESDAY: _____/_____   **MOOD:** _____   **MOON PHASE** ◯

My "I am" Affirmation of the day: _____

Today I am grateful for: _____

I am manifesting: _____

☐ I visualized my dream coming true for 2–5 minutes. ☐ I realized what no longer serves me & imagined my problems healed. ☐ I made time for self-care today.

WEDNESDAY: _____/_____   **MOOD:** _____   **MOON PHASE** ◯

My "I am" Affirmation of the day: _____

Today I am grateful for: _____

I am manifesting: _____

☐ I visualized my dream coming true for 2–5 minutes. ☐ I realized what no longer serves me & imagined my problems healed. ☐ I made time for self-care today.

"Happiness is not a matter of events, it depends upon the tides of the mind." —Alice Meynell

THURSDAY: _____ / _____   **MOOD:** _____   **MOON PHASE** ○

My "I am" Affirmation of the day: _____

Today I am grateful for: _____

I am manifesting: _____

☐ I visualized my dream coming true for 2-5 minutes.   ☐ I realized what no longer serves me & imagined my problems healed.   ☐ I made time for self-care today.

FRIDAY: _____ / _____   **MOOD:** _____   **MOON PHASE** ○

My "I am" Affirmation of the day: _____

Today I am grateful for: _____

I am manifesting: _____

☐ I visualized my dream coming true for 2-5 minutes.   ☐ I realized what no longer serves me & imagined my problems healed.   ☐ I made time for self-care today.

SATURDAY: _____ / _____   **MOOD:** _____   **MOON PHASE** ○

My "I am" Affirmation of the day: _____

Today I am grateful for: _____

I am manifesting: _____

☐ I visualized my dream coming true for 2-5 minutes.   ☐ I realized what no longer serves me & imagined my problems healed.   ☐ I made time for self-care today.

SUNDAY: _____ / _____   **MOOD:** _____   **MOON PHASE** ○

My "I am" Affirmation of the day: _____

Today I am grateful for: _____

I am manifesting: _____

☐ I visualized my dream coming true for 2-5 minutes.   ☐ I realized what no longer serves me & imagined my problems healed.   ☐ I made time for self-care today.

THE BEST THING THAT HAPPENED TO ME THIS WEEK WAS:

week 16

See the true beauty in yourself. Write what you appreciate about yourself—both your external appearance and your personality.

_____

_____

_____

MONDAY: _____ / _____   MOOD: _____   MOON PHASE ◯

My "I am" Affirmation of the day: _____

Today I am grateful for: _____

I am manifesting: _____

☐ I visualized my dream coming true for 2-5 minutes.　　☐ I realized what no longer serves me & imagined my problems healed.　　☐ I made time for self-care today.

TUESDAY: _____ / _____   MOOD: _____   MOON PHASE ◯

My "I am" Affirmation of the day: _____

Today I am grateful for: _____

I am manifesting: _____

☐ I visualized my dream coming true for 2-5 minutes.　　☐ I realized what no longer serves me & imagined my problems healed.　　☐ I made time for self-care today.

WEDNESDAY: _____ / _____   MOOD: _____   MOON PHASE ◯

My "I am" Affirmation of the day: _____

Today I am grateful for: _____

I am manifesting: _____

☐ I visualized my dream coming true for 2-5 minutes.　　☐ I realized what no longer serves me & imagined my problems healed.　　☐ I made time for self-care today.

THURSDAY: _____ / _____   MOOD: _____   MOON PHASE ◯

My "I am" Affirmation of the day: _____

Today I am grateful for: _____

I am manifesting: _____

☐ I visualized my dream   ☐ I realized what no longer serves me   ☐ I made time for
  coming true for 2-5 minutes.   & imagined my problems healed.   self-care today.

FRIDAY: _____ / _____   MOOD: _____   MOON PHASE ◯

My "I am" Affirmation of the day: _____

Today I am grateful for: _____

I am manifesting: _____

☐ I visualized my dream   ☐ I realized what no longer serves me   ☐ I made time for
  coming true for 2-5 minutes.   & imagined my problems healed.   self-care today.

SATURDAY: _____ / _____   MOOD: _____   MOON PHASE ◯

My "I am" Affirmation of the day: _____

Today I am grateful for: _____

I am manifesting: _____

☐ I visualized my dream   ☐ I realized what no longer serves me   ☐ I made time for
  coming true for 2-5 minutes.   & imagined my problems healed.   self-care today.

SUNDAY: _____ / _____   MOOD: _____   MOON PHASE ◯

My "I am" Affirmation of the day: _____

Today I am grateful for: _____

I am manifesting: _____

☐ I visualized my dream   ☐ I realized what no longer serves me   ☐ I made time for
  coming true for 2-5 minutes.   & imagined my problems healed.   self-care today.

THE BEST THING THAT HAPPENED TO ME THIS WEEK WAS:

week 17

Your feelings construct your manifestations. Create some good feelings by writing about the happiest days of your life. As you write them down, take a moment to really feel all the emotions you felt those days. This will help you attract more amazing days and will cultivate gratitude for past experiences.

_____

_____

_____

MONDAY: _____ / _____   **MOOD:** _____   **MOON PHASE** ◯

My "I am" Affirmation of the day: _____

Today I am grateful for: _____

_____

I am manifesting: _____

☐ I visualized my dream coming true for 2-5 minutes.
☐ I realized what no longer serves me & imagined my problems healed.
☐ I made time for self-care today.

TUESDAY: _____ / _____   **MOOD:** _____   **MOON PHASE** ◯

My "I am" Affirmation of the day: _____

Today I am grateful for: _____

_____

I am manifesting: _____

☐ I visualized my dream coming true for 2-5 minutes.
☐ I realized what no longer serves me & imagined my problems healed.
☐ I made time for self-care today.

WEDNESDAY: _____ / _____   **MOOD:** _____   **MOON PHASE** ◯

My "I am" Affirmation of the day: _____

Today I am grateful for: _____

_____

I am manifesting: _____

☐ I visualized my dream coming true for 2-5 minutes.
☐ I realized what no longer serves me & imagined my problems healed.
☐ I made time for self-care today.

"We can change our lives. We can do, have,
and be exactly what we wish." — Anthony Roberts

THURSDAY: _____ / _____   MOOD: _____   MOON PHASE ◯

My "I am" Affirmation of the day: _____
Today I am grateful for: _____
_____
I am manifesting: _____
_____

▢ I visualized my dream coming true for 2-5 minutes.   ▢ I realized what no longer serves me & imagined my problems healed.   ▢ I made time for self-care today.

FRIDAY: _____ / _____   MOOD: _____   MOON PHASE ◯

My "I am" Affirmation of the day: _____
Today I am grateful for: _____
_____
I am manifesting: _____
_____

▢ I visualized my dream coming true for 2-5 minutes.   ▢ I realized what no longer serves me & imagined my problems healed.   ▢ I made time for self-care today.

SATURDAY: _____ / _____   MOOD: _____   MOON PHASE ◯

My "I am" Affirmation of the day: _____
Today I am grateful for: _____
_____
I am manifesting: _____
_____

▢ I visualized my dream coming true for 2-5 minutes.   ▢ I realized what no longer serves me & imagined my problems healed.   ▢ I made time for self-care today.

SUNDAY: _____ / _____   MOOD: _____   MOON PHASE ◯

My "I am" Affirmation of the day: _____
Today I am grateful for: _____
_____
I am manifesting: _____
_____

▢ I visualized my dream coming true for 2-5 minutes.   ▢ I realized what no longer serves me & imagined my problems healed.   ▢ I made time for self-care today.

THE BEST THING THAT HAPPENED TO ME THIS WEEK WAS:

week 18

Gratitude Spree: List everything you are grateful for. Start small with things like your fingertips, your bed, your eyesight, and build to larger things like your best friend and every cent you have in the bank.

_____

_____

_____

MONDAY: ____ / ____   **MOOD:** _____   **MOON PHASE** ⚪

My "I am" Affirmation of the day: _____

Today I am grateful for: _____

I am manifesting: _____

☐ I visualized my dream coming true for 2-5 minutes.   ☐ I realized what no longer serves me & imagined my problems healed.   ☐ I made time for self-care today.

TUESDAY: ____ / ____   **MOOD:** _____   **MOON PHASE** ⚪

My "I am" Affirmation of the day: _____

Today I am grateful for: _____

I am manifesting: _____

☐ I visualized my dream coming true for 2-5 minutes.   ☐ I realized what no longer serves me & imagined my problems healed.   ☐ I made time for self-care today.

WEDNESDAY: ____ / ____   **MOOD:** _____   **MOON PHASE** ⚪

My "I am" Affirmation of the day: _____

Today I am grateful for: _____

I am manifesting: _____

☐ I visualized my dream coming true for 2-5 minutes.   ☐ I realized what no longer serves me & imagined my problems healed.   ☐ I made time for self-care today.

THURSDAY: _____ / _____   **MOOD:** _____   **MOON PHASE** ○

My "I am" Affirmation of the day: _____

Today I am grateful for: _____

I am manifesting: _____

☐ I visualized my dream coming true for 2-5 minutes.   ☐ I realized what no longer serves me & imagined my problems healed.   ☐ I made time for self-care today.

FRIDAY: _____ / _____   **MOOD:** _____   **MOON PHASE** ○

My "I am" Affirmation of the day: _____

Today I am grateful for: _____

I am manifesting: _____

☐ I visualized my dream coming true for 2-5 minutes.   ☐ I realized what no longer serves me & imagined my problems healed.   ☐ I made time for self-care today.

SATURDAY: _____ / _____   **MOOD:** _____   **MOON PHASE** ○

My "I am" Affirmation of the day: _____

Today I am grateful for: _____

I am manifesting: _____

☐ I visualized my dream coming true for 2-5 minutes.   ☐ I realized what no longer serves me & imagined my problems healed.   ☐ I made time for self-care today.

SUNDAY: _____ / _____   **MOOD:** _____   **MOON PHASE** ○

My "I am" Affirmation of the day: _____

Today I am grateful for: _____

I am manifesting: _____

☐ I visualized my dream coming true for 2-5 minutes.   ☐ I realized what no longer serves me & imagined my problems healed.   ☐ I made time for self-care today.

THE BEST THING THAT HAPPENED TO ME THIS WEEK WAS:

IF YOU see someone else achieving what you want, all it means is that it's possible for you to achieve it too. It's the universe showing you that it's on your frequency so celebrate!

Be more mindful. Going forward, as you see people posting about their lives on social media or as you hear others' conversations in real life, really notice how you feel about what they are saying. Are you feeling jealous or wishing you had that? Remember, if you're hearing it or seeing it, it's the universe giving you a sign that it's possible for you. So, honor your feelings but then let them go. Switch your focus to celebrating others' good news. Be genuinely excited for them. Imagine how excited you'd be if that happened to you! Envision it happening to you and know if it is happening for them, it can happen for you, too.

Envision the kind of life you want and then use this space to add or draw pictures to represent your goals and dreams.

week 19

If money were not an issue, you knew you couldn't fail, and all your dreams came true, what would your ideal life be like? Write in the present tense as if you are already living it. Get as detailed as possible to help you gain clarity.

_____

_____

_____

MONDAY: _____ / _____   MOOD: _____   MOON PHASE ○

My "I am" Affirmation of the day: _____

Today I am grateful for: _____

I am manifesting: _____

☐ I visualized my dream coming true for 2-5 minutes.   ☐ I realized what no longer serves me & imagined my problems healed.   ☐ I made time for self-care today.

TUESDAY: _____ / _____   MOOD: _____   MOON PHASE ○

My "I am" Affirmation of the day: _____

Today I am grateful for: _____

I am manifesting: _____

☐ I visualized my dream coming true for 2-5 minutes.   ☐ I realized what no longer serves me & imagined my problems healed.   ☐ I made time for self-care today.

WEDNESDAY: _____ / _____   MOOD: _____   MOON PHASE ○

My "I am" Affirmation of the day: _____

Today I am grateful for: _____

I am manifesting: _____

☐ I visualized my dream coming true for 2-5 minutes.   ☐ I realized what no longer serves me & imagined my problems healed.   ☐ I made time for self-care today.

"The aim of life is to live, and to live means to be aware, joyously, drunkenly, serenely, divinely aware." —Henry Miller

THURSDAY: _____ / _____   **MOOD:** _____   **MOON PHASE** ◯

My "I am" Affirmation of the day: _____

Today I am grateful for: _____

I am manifesting: _____

☐ I visualized my dream   ☐ I realized what no longer serves me   ☐ I made time for
   coming true for 2-5 minutes.   & imagined my problems healed.   self-care today.

FRIDAY: _____ / _____   **MOOD:** _____   **MOON PHASE** ◯

My "I am" Affirmation of the day: _____

Today I am grateful for: _____

I am manifesting: _____

☐ I visualized my dream   ☐ I realized what no longer serves me   ☐ I made time for
   coming true for 2-5 minutes.   & imagined my problems healed.   self-care today.

SATURDAY: _____ / _____   **MOOD:** _____   **MOON PHASE** ◯

My "I am" Affirmation of the day: _____

Today I am grateful for: _____

I am manifesting: _____

☐ I visualized my dream   ☐ I realized what no longer serves me   ☐ I made time for
   coming true for 2-5 minutes.   & imagined my problems healed.   self-care today.

SUNDAY: _____ / _____   **MOOD:** _____   **MOON PHASE** ◯

My "I am" Affirmation of the day: _____

Today I am grateful for: _____

I am manifesting: _____

☐ I visualized my dream   ☐ I realized what no longer serves me   ☐ I made time for
   coming true for 2-5 minutes.   & imagined my problems healed.   self-care today.

THE BEST THING THAT HAPPENED TO ME THIS WEEK WAS:

week 20

It's always great to give yourself space to deeply heal and let go, so it's time to release everything that's bothering you. Write down anything that's currently bringing you down, no matter how small, and then imagine letting it all go. After that, write about the things that you love in your life. Focus on the things that make you smile and make your heart happy.

_____

_____

_____

MONDAY: _____ / _____   **MOOD:** _____   **MOON PHASE** ◯

My "I am" Affirmation of the day: _____

Today I am grateful for: _____

I am manifesting: _____

☐ I visualized my dream coming true for 2-5 minutes. ☐ I realized what no longer serves me & imagined my problems healed. ☐ I made time for self-care today.

TUESDAY: _____ / _____   **MOOD:** _____   **MOON PHASE** ◯

My "I am" Affirmation of the day: _____

Today I am grateful for: _____

I am manifesting: _____

☐ I visualized my dream coming true for 2-5 minutes. ☐ I realized what no longer serves me & imagined my problems healed. ☐ I made time for self-care today.

WEDNESDAY: _____ / _____   **MOOD:** _____   **MOON PHASE** ◯

My "I am" Affirmation of the day: _____

Today I am grateful for: _____

I am manifesting: _____

☐ I visualized my dream coming true for 2-5 minutes. ☐ I realized what no longer serves me & imagined my problems healed. ☐ I made time for self-care today.

THURSDAY: _____ / _____   MOOD: _____   MOON PHASE ⚪

My "I am" Affirmation of the day: _____

Today I am grateful for: _____

I am manifesting: _____

☐ I visualized my dream   ☐ I realized what no longer serves me   ☐ I made time for
   coming true for 2-5 minutes.   & imagined my problems healed.   self-care today.

FRIDAY: _____ / _____   MOOD: _____   MOON PHASE ⚪

My "I am" Affirmation of the day: _____

Today I am grateful for: _____

I am manifesting: _____

☐ I visualized my dream   ☐ I realized what no longer serves me   ☐ I made time for
   coming true for 2-5 minutes.   & imagined my problems healed.   self-care today.

SATURDAY: _____ / _____   MOOD: _____   MOON PHASE ⚪

My "I am" Affirmation of the day: _____

Today I am grateful for: _____

I am manifesting: _____

☐ I visualized my dream   ☐ I realized what no longer serves me   ☐ I made time for
   coming true for 2-5 minutes.   & imagined my problems healed.   self-care today.

SUNDAY: _____ / _____   MOOD: _____   MOON PHASE ⚪

My "I am" Affirmation of the day: _____

Today I am grateful for: _____

I am manifesting: _____

☐ I visualized my dream   ☐ I realized what no longer serves me   ☐ I made time for
   coming true for 2-5 minutes.   & imagined my problems healed.   self-care today.

THE BEST THING THAT HAPPENED TO ME THIS WEEK WAS:

week 21

A fairy godmother is granting you three wishes. What would they be? She's also letting you grant one wish to everyone you love. What would they be? After each, take a moment to really envision it happening for yourself and the others.

_____

_____

_____

MONDAY: _____ / _____   **MOOD:** _____   **MOON PHASE** ◯

My "I am" Affirmation of the day: _____

Today I am grateful for: _____

I am manifesting: _____

| ☐ I visualized my dream coming true for 2-5 minutes. | ☐ I realized what no longer serves me & imagined my problems healed. | ☐ I made time for self-care today. |

TUESDAY: _____ / _____   **MOOD:** _____   **MOON PHASE** ◯

My "I am" Affirmation of the day: _____

Today I am grateful for: _____

I am manifesting: _____

| ☐ I visualized my dream coming true for 2-5 minutes. | ☐ I realized what no longer serves me & imagined my problems healed. | ☐ I made time for self-care today. |

WEDNESDAY: _____ / _____   **MOOD:** _____   **MOON PHASE** ◯

My "I am" Affirmation of the day: _____

Today I am grateful for: _____

I am manifesting: _____

| ☐ I visualized my dream coming true for 2-5 minutes. | ☐ I realized what no longer serves me & imagined my problems healed. | ☐ I made time for self-care today. |

"Happiness resides not in possessions, and not in gold,
happiness dwells in the soul." —Democritus

THURSDAY: _____ / _____   **MOOD:** _____   **MOON PHASE** ◯

My "I am" Affirmation of the day: _____

Today I am grateful for: _____

I am manifesting: _____

☐ I visualized my dream coming true for 2-5 minutes.   ☐ I realized what no longer serves me & imagined my problems healed.   ☐ I made time for self-care today.

FRIDAY: _____ / _____   **MOOD:** _____   **MOON PHASE** ◯

My "I am" Affirmation of the day: _____

Today I am grateful for: _____

I am manifesting: _____

☐ I visualized my dream coming true for 2-5 minutes.   ☐ I realized what no longer serves me & imagined my problems healed.   ☐ I made time for self-care today.

SATURDAY: _____ / _____   **MOOD:** _____   **MOON PHASE** ◯

My "I am" Affirmation of the day: _____

Today I am grateful for: _____

I am manifesting: _____

☐ I visualized my dream coming true for 2-5 minutes.   ☐ I realized what no longer serves me & imagined my problems healed.   ☐ I made time for self-care today.

SUNDAY: _____ / _____   **MOOD:** _____   **MOON PHASE** ◯

My "I am" Affirmation of the day: _____

Today I am grateful for: _____

I am manifesting: _____

☐ I visualized my dream coming true for 2-5 minutes.   ☐ I realized what no longer serves me & imagined my problems healed.   ☐ I made time for self-care today.

THE BEST THING THAT HAPPENED TO ME THIS WEEK WAS:

week 22

See the true beauty in yourself. Write what you appreciate about yourself—both your external appearance and your personality.

_____

_____

_____

MONDAY: _____ / _____   **MOOD:** _____   **MOON PHASE** ○

My "I am" Affirmation of the day: _____

Today I am grateful for: _____

I am manifesting: _____

▢ I visualized my dream coming true for 2-5 minutes.   ▢ I realized what no longer serves me & imagined my problems healed.   ▢ I made time for self-care today.

TUESDAY: _____ / _____   **MOOD:** _____   **MOON PHASE** ○

My "I am" Affirmation of the day: _____

Today I am grateful for: _____

I am manifesting: _____

▢ I visualized my dream coming true for 2-5 minutes.   ▢ I realized what no longer serves me & imagined my problems healed.   ▢ I made time for self-care today.

WEDNESDAY: _____ / _____   **MOOD:** _____   **MOON PHASE** ○

My "I am" Affirmation of the day: _____

Today I am grateful for: _____

I am manifesting: _____

▢ I visualized my dream coming true for 2-5 minutes.   ▢ I realized what no longer serves me & imagined my problems healed.   ▢ I made time for self-care today.

THURSDAY: _____ / _____   **MOOD:** _____   **MOON PHASE** ○

My "I am" Affirmation of the day: _____

Today I am grateful for: _____

I am manifesting: _____

☐ I visualized my dream coming true for 2-5 minutes.   ☐ I realized what no longer serves me & imagined my problems healed.   ☐ I made time for self-care today.

FRIDAY: _____ / _____   **MOOD:** _____   **MOON PHASE** ○

My "I am" Affirmation of the day: _____

Today I am grateful for: _____

I am manifesting: _____

☐ I visualized my dream coming true for 2-5 minutes.   ☐ I realized what no longer serves me & imagined my problems healed.   ☐ I made time for self-care today.

SATURDAY: _____ / _____   **MOOD:** _____   **MOON PHASE** ○

My "I am" Affirmation of the day: _____

Today I am grateful for: _____

I am manifesting: _____

☐ I visualized my dream coming true for 2-5 minutes.   ☐ I realized what no longer serves me & imagined my problems healed.   ☐ I made time for self-care today.

SUNDAY: _____ / _____   **MOOD:** _____   **MOON PHASE** ○

My "I am" Affirmation of the day: _____

Today I am grateful for: _____

I am manifesting: _____

☐ I visualized my dream coming true for 2-5 minutes.   ☐ I realized what no longer serves me & imagined my problems healed.   ☐ I made time for self-care today.

THE BEST THING THAT HAPPENED TO ME THIS WEEK WAS:

week 23

Your feelings construct your manifestations. Create some good feelings by writing about the happiest days of your life. As you write them down, take a moment to really feel all the emotions you felt those days. This will help you attract more amazing days and will cultivate gratitude for past experiences.

_____

_____

_____

monday: ____ / ____   mood: _____   moon phase ◯

My "I am" Affirmation of the day: _____

Today I am grateful for: _____

I am manifesting: _____

☐ I visualized my dream coming true for 2-5 minutes.   ☐ I realized what no longer serves me & imagined my problems healed.   ☐ I made time for self-care today.

tuesday: ____ / ____   mood: _____   moon phase ◯

My "I am" Affirmation of the day: _____

Today I am grateful for: _____

I am manifesting: _____

☐ I visualized my dream coming true for 2-5 minutes.   ☐ I realized what no longer serves me & imagined my problems healed.   ☐ I made time for self-care today.

wednesday: ____ / ____   mood: _____   moon phase ◯

My "I am" Affirmation of the day: _____

Today I am grateful for: _____

I am manifesting: _____

☐ I visualized my dream coming true for 2-5 minutes.   ☐ I realized what no longer serves me & imagined my problems healed.   ☐ I made time for self-care today.

"It's time to start living the life you've imagined." —Henry James

THURSDAY: _____ / _____ **MOOD:** _____ **MOON PHASE** ◯

My "I am" Affirmation of the day: _____

Today I am grateful for: _____

I am manifesting: _____

☐ I visualized my dream coming true for 2-5 minutes. ☐ I realized what no longer serves me & imagined my problems healed. ☐ I made time for self-care today.

FRIDAY: _____ / _____ **MOOD:** _____ **MOON PHASE** ◯

My "I am" Affirmation of the day: _____

Today I am grateful for: _____

I am manifesting: _____

☐ I visualized my dream coming true for 2-5 minutes. ☐ I realized what no longer serves me & imagined my problems healed. ☐ I made time for self-care today.

SATURDAY: _____ / _____ **MOOD:** _____ **MOON PHASE** ◯

My "I am" Affirmation of the day: _____

Today I am grateful for: _____

I am manifesting: _____

☐ I visualized my dream coming true for 2-5 minutes. ☐ I realized what no longer serves me & imagined my problems healed. ☐ I made time for self-care today.

SUNDAY: _____ / _____ **MOOD:** _____ **MOON PHASE** ◯

My "I am" Affirmation of the day: _____

Today I am grateful for: _____

I am manifesting: _____

☐ I visualized my dream coming true for 2-5 minutes. ☐ I realized what no longer serves me & imagined my problems healed. ☐ I made time for self-care today.

THE BEST THING THAT HAPPENED TO ME THIS WEEK WAS:

week 24

Gratitude Spree: List everything you are grateful for. Start small with things like your fingertips, your bed, your eyesight, and build to larger things like your best friend and every cent you have in the bank.

_____

_____

_____

MONDAY: _____ / _____ **MOOD:** _____ **MOON PHASE** ◯

My "I am" Affirmation of the day: _____

Today I am grateful for: _____

I am manifesting: _____

▢ I visualized my dream coming true for 2-5 minutes. ▢ I realized what no longer serves me & imagined my problems healed. ▢ I made time for self-care today.

TUESDAY: _____ / _____ **MOOD:** _____ **MOON PHASE** ◯

My "I am" Affirmation of the day: _____

Today I am grateful for: _____

I am manifesting: _____

▢ I visualized my dream coming true for 2-5 minutes. ▢ I realized what no longer serves me & imagined my problems healed. ▢ I made time for self-care today.

WEDNESDAY: _____ / _____ **MOOD:** _____ **MOON PHASE** ◯

My "I am" Affirmation of the day: _____

Today I am grateful for: _____

I am manifesting: _____

▢ I visualized my dream coming true for 2-5 minutes. ▢ I realized what no longer serves me & imagined my problems healed. ▢ I made time for self-care today.

THURSDAY: _____ / _____   **MOOD:** _____   **MOON PHASE** ○

My "I am" Affirmation of the day: _____

Today I am grateful for: _____

I am manifesting: _____

☐ I visualized my dream coming true for 2-5 minutes.   ☐ I realized what no longer serves me & imagined my problems healed.   ☐ I made time for self-care today.

FRIDAY: _____ / _____   **MOOD:** _____   **MOON PHASE** ○

My "I am" Affirmation of the day: _____

Today I am grateful for: _____

I am manifesting: _____

☐ I visualized my dream coming true for 2-5 minutes.   ☐ I realized what no longer serves me & imagined my problems healed.   ☐ I made time for self-care today.

SATURDAY: _____ / _____   **MOOD:** _____   **MOON PHASE** ○

My "I am" Affirmation of the day: _____

Today I am grateful for: _____

I am manifesting: _____

☐ I visualized my dream coming true for 2-5 minutes.   ☐ I realized what no longer serves me & imagined my problems healed.   ☐ I made time for self-care today.

SUNDAY: _____ / _____   **MOOD:** _____   **MOON PHASE** ○

My "I am" Affirmation of the day: _____

Today I am grateful for: _____

I am manifesting: _____

☐ I visualized my dream coming true for 2-5 minutes.   ☐ I realized what no longer serves me & imagined my problems healed.   ☐ I made time for self-care today.

THE BEST THING THAT HAPPENED TO ME THIS WEEK WAS:

YOU are TALENTED enough. YOU are CAPABLE enough. YOU are WORTHY enough. YOU can DO ANYTHING!

take a moment to think about everything you've already achieved. I guarantee you, there are more things than you are giving yourself credit for. Think of all the talents you possess, honor them, feel grateful for them. Now, remember, all those things you already achieved were once dreams in your head. If you were able to achieve all of that, why can't you achieve your current dreams? YOU GOT THIS!

Write about an achievement you're most proud of.

week 25

If money were not an issue, you knew you couldn't fail, and all your dreams came true, what would your ideal life be like? Write in the present tense as if you are already living it. Get as detailed as possible to help you gain clarity.

_____

_____

_____

MONDAY: _____ / _____   MOOD: _____   MOON PHASE ⚪

My "I am" Affirmation of the day: _____

Today I am grateful for: _____

I am manifesting: _____

☐ I visualized my dream coming true for 2-5 minutes.　☐ I realized what no longer serves me & imagined my problems healed.　☐ I made time for self-care today.

TUESDAY: _____ / _____   MOOD: _____   MOON PHASE ⚪

My "I am" Affirmation of the day: _____

Today I am grateful for: _____

I am manifesting: _____

☐ I visualized my dream coming true for 2-5 minutes.　☐ I realized what no longer serves me & imagined my problems healed.　☐ I made time for self-care today.

WEDNESDAY: _____ / _____   MOOD: _____   MOON PHASE ⚪

My "I am" Affirmation of the day: _____

Today I am grateful for: _____

I am manifesting: _____

☐ I visualized my dream coming true for 2-5 minutes.　☐ I realized what no longer serves me & imagined my problems healed.　☐ I made time for self-care today.

"Don't let life discourage you; everyone who got where he is had to begin where he was." —Richard Evans

THURSDAY: _____ / _____   **MOOD:** _____   **MOON PHASE** ◯

My "I am" Affirmation of the day: _____

Today I am grateful for: _____
_____

I am manifesting: _____
_____

⬜ I visualized my dream coming true for 2-5 minutes.   ⬜ I realized what no longer serves me & imagined my problems healed.   ⬜ I made time for self-care today.

FRIDAY: _____ / _____   **MOOD:** _____   **MOON PHASE** ◯

My "I am" Affirmation of the day: _____

Today I am grateful for: _____
_____

I am manifesting: _____
_____

⬜ I visualized my dream coming true for 2-5 minutes.   ⬜ I realized what no longer serves me & imagined my problems healed.   ⬜ I made time for self-care today.

SATURDAY: _____ / _____   **MOOD:** _____   **MOON PHASE** ◯

My "I am" Affirmation of the day: _____

Today I am grateful for: _____
_____

I am manifesting: _____
_____

⬜ I visualized my dream coming true for 2-5 minutes.   ⬜ I realized what no longer serves me & imagined my problems healed.   ⬜ I made time for self-care today.

SUNDAY: _____ / _____   **MOOD:** _____   **MOON PHASE** ◯

My "I am" Affirmation of the day: _____

Today I am grateful for: _____
_____

I am manifesting: _____
_____

⬜ I visualized my dream coming true for 2-5 minutes.   ⬜ I realized what no longer serves me & imagined my problems healed.   ⬜ I made time for self-care today.

THE BEST THING THAT HAPPENED TO ME THIS WEEK WAS:

week 26

It's always great to give yourself space to deeply heal and let go, so it's time to release everything that's bothering you. Write down anything that's currently bringing you down, no matter how small, and then imagine letting it all go. After that, write about the things that you love in your life. Focus on the things that make you smile and make your heart happy.

_____

_____

_____

MONDAY: _____ / _____   **MOOD:** _____   **MOON PHASE** ◯

My "I am" Affirmation of the day: _____

Today I am grateful for: _____

_____

I am manifesting: _____

☐ I visualized my dream coming true for 2-5 minutes.   ☐ I realized what no longer serves me & imagined my problems healed.   ☐ I made time for self-care today.

TUESDAY: _____ / _____   **MOOD:** _____   **MOON PHASE** ◯

My "I am" Affirmation of the day: _____

Today I am grateful for: _____

_____

I am manifesting: _____

☐ I visualized my dream coming true for 2-5 minutes.   ☐ I realized what no longer serves me & imagined my problems healed.   ☐ I made time for self-care today.

WEDNESDAY: _____ / _____   **MOOD:** _____   **MOON PHASE** ◯

My "I am" Affirmation of the day: _____

Today I am grateful for: _____

_____

I am manifesting: _____

☐ I visualized my dream coming true for 2-5 minutes.   ☐ I realized what no longer serves me & imagined my problems healed.   ☐ I made time for self-care today.

THURSDAY: _____ / _____   **MOOD:** _____   **MOON PHASE** ◯

My "I am" Affirmation of the day: _____

Today I am grateful for: _____

I am manifesting: _____

☐ I visualized my dream coming true for 2-5 minutes.   ☐ I realized what no longer serves me & imagined my problems healed.   ☐ I made time for self-care today.

FRIDAY: _____ / _____   **MOOD:** _____   **MOON PHASE** ◯

My "I am" Affirmation of the day: _____

Today I am grateful for: _____

I am manifesting: _____

☐ I visualized my dream coming true for 2-5 minutes.   ☐ I realized what no longer serves me & imagined my problems healed.   ☐ I made time for self-care today.

SATURDAY: _____ / _____   **MOOD:** _____   **MOON PHASE** ◯

My "I am" Affirmation of the day: _____

Today I am grateful for: _____

I am manifesting: _____

☐ I visualized my dream coming true for 2-5 minutes.   ☐ I realized what no longer serves me & imagined my problems healed.   ☐ I made time for self-care today.

SUNDAY: _____ / _____   **MOOD:** _____   **MOON PHASE** ◯

My "I am" Affirmation of the day: _____

Today I am grateful for: _____

I am manifesting: _____

☐ I visualized my dream coming true for 2-5 minutes.   ☐ I realized what no longer serves me & imagined my problems healed.   ☐ I made time for self-care today.

THE BEST THING THAT HAPPENED TO ME THIS WEEK WAS:

week 27

A fairy godmother is granting you three wishes. What would they be? She's also letting you grant one wish to everyone you love. What would they be? After each, take a moment to really envision it happening for yourself and the others.

_____

_____

_____

MONDAY: _____/_____   **MOOD:** _____   MOON PHASE ○

My "I am" Affirmation of the day: _____

Today I am grateful for: _____

I am manifesting: _____

☐ I visualized my dream coming true for 2-5 minutes.   ☐ I realized what no longer serves me & imagined my problems healed.   ☐ I made time for self-care today.

TUESDAY: _____/_____   **MOOD:** _____   MOON PHASE ○

My "I am" Affirmation of the day: _____

Today I am grateful for: _____

I am manifesting: _____

☐ I visualized my dream coming true for 2-5 minutes.   ☐ I realized what no longer serves me & imagined my problems healed.   ☐ I made time for self-care today.

WEDNESDAY: _____/_____   **MOOD:** _____   MOON PHASE ○

My "I am" Affirmation of the day: _____

Today I am grateful for: _____

I am manifesting: _____

☐ I visualized my dream coming true for 2-5 minutes.   ☐ I realized what no longer serves me & imagined my problems healed.   ☐ I made time for self-care today.

"Never tell me the sky is the limit when there are footprints on the moon." —Author Unknown

THURSDAY: _____ / _____   **MOOD:** _____   **MOON PHASE** ◯

My "I am" Affirmation of the day: _____

Today I am grateful for: _____

_____

I am manifesting: _____

☐ I visualized my dream coming true for 2-5 minutes.　　☐ I realized what no longer serves me & imagined my problems healed.　　☐ I made time for self-care today.

FRIDAY: _____ / _____   **MOOD:** _____   **MOON PHASE** ◯

My "I am" Affirmation of the day: _____

Today I am grateful for: _____

_____

I am manifesting: _____

☐ I visualized my dream coming true for 2-5 minutes.　　☐ I realized what no longer serves me & imagined my problems healed.　　☐ I made time for self-care today.

SATURDAY: _____ / _____   **MOOD:** _____   **MOON PHASE** ◯

My "I am" Affirmation of the day: _____

Today I am grateful for: _____

_____

I am manifesting: _____

☐ I visualized my dream coming true for 2-5 minutes.　　☐ I realized what no longer serves me & imagined my problems healed.　　☐ I made time for self-care today.

SUNDAY: _____ / _____   **MOOD:** _____   **MOON PHASE** ◯

My "I am" Affirmation of the day: _____

Today I am grateful for: _____

_____

I am manifesting: _____

☐ I visualized my dream coming true for 2-5 minutes.　　☐ I realized what no longer serves me & imagined my problems healed.　　☐ I made time for self-care today.

THE BEST THING THAT HAPPENED TO ME THIS WEEK WAS:

weeĸ 28

See the true beauty in yourself. Write what you appreciate about yourself—both your external appearance and your personality.

_____

_____

_____

monDaY: ____/____   mooD: _____   moon pHase ◯

My "I am" Affirmation of the day: _____

Today I am grateful for: _____

I am manifesting: _____

| ☐ | I visualized my dream coming true for 2-5 minutes. | ☐ | I realized what no longer serves me & imagined my problems healed. | ☐ | I made time for self-care today. |

TUesDaY: ____/____   mooD: _____   moon pHase ◯

My "I am" Affirmation of the day: _____

Today I am grateful for: _____

I am manifesting: _____

| ☐ | I visualized my dream coming true for 2-5 minutes. | ☐ | I realized what no longer serves me & imagined my problems healed. | ☐ | I made time for self-care today. |

weDnesDaY: ____/____   mooD: _____   moon pHase ◯

My "I am" Affirmation of the day: _____

Today I am grateful for: _____

I am manifesting: _____

| ☐ | I visualized my dream coming true for 2-5 minutes. | ☐ | I realized what no longer serves me & imagined my problems healed. | ☐ | I made time for self-care today. |

THURSDAY: _____ / _____   **MOOD:** _____   **MOON PHASE** ◯

My "I am" Affirmation of the day: _____
Today I am grateful for: _____

I am manifesting: _____

☐ I visualized my dream coming true for 2-5 minutes.   ☐ I realized what no longer serves me & imagined my problems healed.   ☐ I made time for self-care today.

FRIDAY: _____ / _____   **MOOD:** _____   **MOON PHASE** ◯

My "I am" Affirmation of the day: _____
Today I am grateful for: _____

I am manifesting: _____

☐ I visualized my dream coming true for 2-5 minutes.   ☐ I realized what no longer serves me & imagined my problems healed.   ☐ I made time for self-care today.

SATURDAY: _____ / _____   **MOOD:** _____   **MOON PHASE** ◯

My "I am" Affirmation of the day: _____
Today I am grateful for: _____

I am manifesting: _____

☐ I visualized my dream coming true for 2-5 minutes.   ☐ I realized what no longer serves me & imagined my problems healed.   ☐ I made time for self-care today.

SUNDAY: _____ / _____   **MOOD:** _____   **MOON PHASE** ◯

My "I am" Affirmation of the day: _____
Today I am grateful for: _____

I am manifesting: _____

☐ I visualized my dream coming true for 2-5 minutes.   ☐ I realized what no longer serves me & imagined my problems healed.   ☐ I made time for self-care today.

THE BEST THING THAT HAPPENED TO ME THIS WEEK WAS:

week 29

Your feelings construct your manifestations. Create some good feelings by writing about the happiest days of your life. As you write them down, take a moment to really feel all the emotions you felt those days. This will help you attract more amazing days and will cultivate gratitude for past experiences.

_____

_____

_____

MONDAY: _____ / _____ **MOOD:** _____ **MOON PHASE** ⚪

My "I am" Affirmation of the day: _____

Today I am grateful for: _____

I am manifesting: _____

☐ I visualized my dream coming true for 2-5 minutes. ☐ I realized what no longer serves me & imagined my problems healed. ☐ I made time for self-care today.

TUESDAY: _____ / _____ **MOOD:** _____ **MOON PHASE** ⚪

My "I am" Affirmation of the day: _____

Today I am grateful for: _____

I am manifesting: _____

☐ I visualized my dream coming true for 2-5 minutes. ☐ I realized what no longer serves me & imagined my problems healed. ☐ I made time for self-care today.

WEDNESDAY: _____ / _____ **MOOD:** _____ **MOON PHASE** ⚪

My "I am" Affirmation of the day: _____

Today I am grateful for: _____

I am manifesting: _____

☐ I visualized my dream coming true for 2-5 minutes. ☐ I realized what no longer serves me & imagined my problems healed. ☐ I made time for self-care today.

"Never fear shadows. They simply mean there's a light shining somewhere nearby." —Ruth E. Renkel

THURSDAY: _____ / _____   **MOOD:** _____   **MOON PHASE** ◯

My "I am" Affirmation of the day: _____

Today I am grateful for: _____

I am manifesting: _____

☐ I visualized my dream coming true for 2-5 minutes.   ☐ I realized what no longer serves me & imagined my problems healed.   ☐ I made time for self-care today.

FRIDAY: _____ / _____   **MOOD:** _____   **MOON PHASE** ◯

My "I am" Affirmation of the day: _____

Today I am grateful for: _____

I am manifesting: _____

☐ I visualized my dream coming true for 2-5 minutes.   ☐ I realized what no longer serves me & imagined my problems healed.   ☐ I made time for self-care today.

SATURDAY: _____ / _____   **MOOD:** _____   **MOON PHASE** ◯

My "I am" Affirmation of the day: _____

Today I am grateful for: _____

I am manifesting: _____

☐ I visualized my dream coming true for 2-5 minutes.   ☐ I realized what no longer serves me & imagined my problems healed.   ☐ I made time for self-care today.

SUNDAY: _____ / _____   **MOOD:** _____   **MOON PHASE** ◯

My "I am" Affirmation of the day: _____

Today I am grateful for: _____

I am manifesting: _____

☐ I visualized my dream coming true for 2-5 minutes.   ☐ I realized what no longer serves me & imagined my problems healed.   ☐ I made time for self-care today.

THE BEST THING THAT HAPPENED TO ME THIS WEEK WAS:

week 30

Gratitude Spree: List everything you are grateful for. Start small with things like your fingertips, your bed, your eyesight, and build to larger things like your best friend and every cent you have in the bank.

_____

_____

_____

monday: ____ / ____   **mood:** _____   **moon phase** ○

My "I am" Affirmation of the day: _____

Today I am grateful for: _____

I am manifesting: _____

☐ I visualized my dream coming true for 2-5 minutes. ☐ I realized what no longer serves me & imagined my problems healed. ☐ I made time for self-care today.

tuesday: ____ / ____   **mood:** _____   **moon phase** ○

My "I am" Affirmation of the day: _____

Today I am grateful for: _____

I am manifesting: _____

☐ I visualized my dream coming true for 2-5 minutes. ☐ I realized what no longer serves me & imagined my problems healed. ☐ I made time for self-care today.

wednesday: ____ / ____   **mood:** _____   **moon phase** ○

My "I am" Affirmation of the day: _____

Today I am grateful for: _____

I am manifesting: _____

☐ I visualized my dream coming true for 2-5 minutes. ☐ I realized what no longer serves me & imagined my problems healed. ☐ I made time for self-care today.

THURSDAY: _____ / _____   **MOOD:** _____   **MOON PHASE** ◯

My "I am" Affirmation of the day: _____

Today I am grateful for: _____

I am manifesting: _____

☐ I visualized my dream coming true for 2-5 minutes.   ☐ I realized what no longer serves me & imagined my problems healed.   ☐ I made time for self-care today.

FRIDAY: _____ / _____   **MOOD:** _____   **MOON PHASE** ◯

My "I am" Affirmation of the day: _____

Today I am grateful for: _____

I am manifesting: _____

☐ I visualized my dream coming true for 2-5 minutes.   ☐ I realized what no longer serves me & imagined my problems healed.   ☐ I made time for self-care today.

SATURDAY: _____ / _____   **MOOD:** _____   **MOON PHASE** ◯

My "I am" Affirmation of the day: _____

Today I am grateful for: _____

I am manifesting: _____

☐ I visualized my dream coming true for 2-5 minutes.   ☐ I realized what no longer serves me & imagined my problems healed.   ☐ I made time for self-care today.

SUNDAY: _____ / _____   **MOOD:** _____   **MOON PHASE** ◯

My "I am" Affirmation of the day: _____

Today I am grateful for: _____

I am manifesting: _____

☐ I visualized my dream coming true for 2-5 minutes.   ☐ I realized what no longer serves me & imagined my problems healed.   ☐ I made time for self-care today.

THE BEST THING THAT HAPPENED TO ME THIS WEEK WAS:

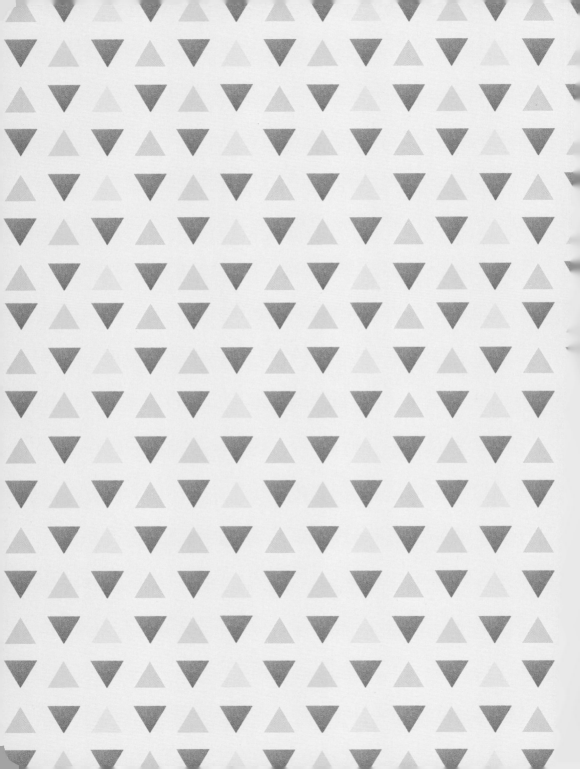

spread some kindness today!

YOU are SO WONDERFUL anD SO are THE PEOPLE YOU LOVE MOST. THINK ABOUT THOSE PRECIOUS SOULS IN YOUR LIFE anD THINK ABOUT WHY YOU LOVE THEM SO MUCH. WHAT MAKES THEM SO AMAZING? WHY are YOU GRATEFUL TO HAVE THEM IN YOUR LIFE? WHEN YOU'RE DONE THINKING ABOUT IT – ACTUALLY TELL THEM!

Brainstorm some ideas for performing small acts of kindness. Call a friend, buy a stranger coffee, or cook a meal for your neighbor.

week 31

A fairy godmother is granting you three wishes. What would they be? She's also letting you grant one wish to everyone you love. What would they be? After each, take a moment to really envision it happening for yourself and the others.

_____

_____

_____

MONDAY: _____ / _____   MOOD: _____   MOON PHASE ◯

My "I am" Affirmation of the day: _____

Today I am grateful for: _____

I am manifesting: _____

☐ I visualized my dream coming true for 2-5 minutes.　　☐ I realized what no longer serves me & imagined my problems healed.　　☐ I made time for self-care today.

TUESDAY: _____ / _____   MOOD: _____   MOON PHASE ◯

My "I am" Affirmation of the day: _____

Today I am grateful for: _____

I am manifesting: _____

☐ I visualized my dream coming true for 2-5 minutes.　　☐ I realized what no longer serves me & imagined my problems healed.　　☐ I made time for self-care today.

WEDNESDAY: _____ / _____   MOOD: _____   MOON PHASE ◯

My "I am" Affirmation of the day: _____

Today I am grateful for: _____

I am manifesting: _____

☐ I visualized my dream coming true for 2-5 minutes.　　☐ I realized what no longer serves me & imagined my problems healed.　　☐ I made time for self-care today.

"Your success and happiness lie in you." —Helen Keller

THURSDAY: _____ / _____   **MOOD:** _____   **MOON PHASE** ◯

My "I am" Affirmation of the day: _____

Today I am grateful for: _____

I am manifesting: _____

☐ I visualized my dream coming true for 2-5 minutes.   ☐ I realized what no longer serves me & imagined my problems healed.   ☐ I made time for self-care today.

FRIDAY: _____ / _____   **MOOD:** _____   **MOON PHASE** ◯

My "I am" Affirmation of the day: _____

Today I am grateful for: _____

I am manifesting: _____

☐ I visualized my dream coming true for 2-5 minutes.   ☐ I realized what no longer serves me & imagined my problems healed.   ☐ I made time for self-care today.

SATURDAY: _____ / _____   **MOOD:** _____   **MOON PHASE** ◯

My "I am" Affirmation of the day: _____

Today I am grateful for: _____

I am manifesting: _____

☐ I visualized my dream coming true for 2-5 minutes.   ☐ I realized what no longer serves me & imagined my problems healed.   ☐ I made time for self-care today.

SUNDAY: _____ / _____   **MOOD:** _____   **MOON PHASE** ◯

My "I am" Affirmation of the day: _____

Today I am grateful for: _____

I am manifesting: _____

☐ I visualized my dream coming true for 2-5 minutes.   ☐ I realized what no longer serves me & imagined my problems healed.   ☐ I made time for self-care today.

THE BEST THING THAT HAPPENED TO ME THIS WEEK WAS:

week 32

See the true beauty in yourself. Write what you appreciate about yourself—both your external appearance and your personality.

_____

_____

_____

MONDAY: _____ / _____   MOOD: _____   MOON PHASE ○

My "I am" Affirmation of the day: _____

Today I am grateful for: _____

I am manifesting: _____

☐ I visualized my dream coming true for 2-5 minutes. ☐ I realized what no longer serves me & imagined my problems healed. ☐ I made time for self-care today.

TUESDAY: _____ / _____   MOOD: _____   MOON PHASE ○

My "I am" Affirmation of the day: _____

Today I am grateful for: _____

I am manifesting: _____

☐ I visualized my dream coming true for 2-5 minutes. ☐ I realized what no longer serves me & imagined my problems healed. ☐ I made time for self-care today.

WEDNESDAY: _____ / _____   MOOD: _____   MOON PHASE ○

My "I am" Affirmation of the day: _____

Today I am grateful for: _____

I am manifesting: _____

☐ I visualized my dream coming true for 2-5 minutes. ☐ I realized what no longer serves me & imagined my problems healed. ☐ I made time for self-care today.

THURSDAY: _____ / _____   **MOOD:** _____   **MOON PHASE** ◯

My "I am" Affirmation of the day: _____

Today I am grateful for: _____

I am manifesting: _____

☐ I visualized my dream coming true for 2-5 minutes.   ☐ I realized what no longer serves me & imagined my problems healed.   ☐ I made time for self-care today.

FRIDAY: _____ / _____   **MOOD:** _____   **MOON PHASE** ◯

My "I am" Affirmation of the day: _____

Today I am grateful for: _____

I am manifesting: _____

☐ I visualized my dream coming true for 2-5 minutes.   ☐ I realized what no longer serves me & imagined my problems healed.   ☐ I made time for self-care today.

SATURDAY: _____ / _____   **MOOD:** _____   **MOON PHASE** ◯

My "I am" Affirmation of the day: _____

Today I am grateful for: _____

I am manifesting: _____

☐ I visualized my dream coming true for 2-5 minutes.   ☐ I realized what no longer serves me & imagined my problems healed.   ☐ I made time for self-care today.

SUNDAY: _____ / _____   **MOOD:** _____   **MOON PHASE** ◯

My "I am" Affirmation of the day: _____

Today I am grateful for: _____

I am manifesting: _____

☐ I visualized my dream coming true for 2-5 minutes.   ☐ I realized what no longer serves me & imagined my problems healed.   ☐ I made time for self-care today.

THE BEST THING THAT HAPPENED TO ME THIS WEEK WAS:

week 33

A fairy godmother is granting you three wishes. What would they be? She's also letting you grant one wish to everyone you love. What would they be? After each, take a moment to really envision it happening for yourself and the others.

_____

_____

_____

MONDAY: ____/____   MOOD: _____   MOON PHASE ◯

My "I am" Affirmation of the day: _____

Today I am grateful for: _____

I am manifesting: _____

☐ I visualized my dream coming true for 2-5 minutes.   ☐ I realized what no longer serves me & imagined my problems healed.   ☐ I made time for self-care today.

TUESDAY: ____/____   MOOD: _____   MOON PHASE ◯

My "I am" Affirmation of the day: _____

Today I am grateful for: _____

I am manifesting: _____

☐ I visualized my dream coming true for 2-5 minutes.   ☐ I realized what no longer serves me & imagined my problems healed.   ☐ I made time for self-care today.

WEDNESDAY: ____/____   MOOD: _____   MOON PHASE ◯

My "I am" Affirmation of the day: _____

Today I am grateful for: _____

I am manifesting: _____

☐ I visualized my dream coming true for 2-5 minutes.   ☐ I realized what no longer serves me & imagined my problems healed.   ☐ I made time for self-care today.

"The secret to happiness is freedom. And the secret to freedom is courage." —Thucydides

THURSDAY: _____ / _____ **MOOD:** _____ **MOON PHASE** ◯

My "I am" Affirmation of the day: _____

Today I am grateful for: _____

I am manifesting: _____

☐ I visualized my dream coming true for 2-5 minutes.   ☐ I realized what no longer serves me & imagined my problems healed.   ☐ I made time for self-care today.

FRIDAY: _____ / _____ **MOOD:** _____ **MOON PHASE** ◯

My "I am" Affirmation of the day: _____

Today I am grateful for: _____

I am manifesting: _____

☐ I visualized my dream coming true for 2-5 minutes.   ☐ I realized what no longer serves me & imagined my problems healed.   ☐ I made time for self-care today.

SATURDAY: _____ / _____ **MOOD:** _____ **MOON PHASE** ◯

My "I am" Affirmation of the day: _____

Today I am grateful for: _____

I am manifesting: _____

☐ I visualized my dream coming true for 2-5 minutes.   ☐ I realized what no longer serves me & imagined my problems healed.   ☐ I made time for self-care today.

SUNDAY: _____ / _____ **MOOD:** _____ **MOON PHASE** ◯

My "I am" Affirmation of the day: _____

Today I am grateful for: _____

I am manifesting: _____

☐ I visualized my dream coming true for 2-5 minutes.   ☐ I realized what no longer serves me & imagined my problems healed.   ☐ I made time for self-care today.

THE BEST THING THAT HAPPENED TO ME THIS WEEK WAS:

week 34

See the true beauty in yourself. Write what you appreciate about yourself—both your external appearance and your personality.

_____

_____

_____

MONDAY: _____ / _____   MOOD: _____   MOON PHASE ◯

My "I am" Affirmation of the day: _____
Today I am grateful for: _____

I am manifesting: _____

☐ I visualized my dream coming true for 2-5 minutes.   ☐ I realized what no longer serves me & imagined my problems healed.   ☐ I made time for self-care today.

TUESDAY: _____ / _____   MOOD: _____   MOON PHASE ◯

My "I am" Affirmation of the day: _____
Today I am grateful for: _____

I am manifesting: _____

☐ I visualized my dream coming true for 2-5 minutes.   ☐ I realized what no longer serves me & imagined my problems healed.   ☐ I made time for self-care today.

WEDNESDAY: _____ / _____   MOOD: _____   MOON PHASE ◯

My "I am" Affirmation of the day: _____
Today I am grateful for: _____

I am manifesting: _____

☐ I visualized my dream coming true for 2-5 minutes.   ☐ I realized what no longer serves me & imagined my problems healed.   ☐ I made time for self-care today.

THURSDAY: _____ / _____   **MOOD:** _____   **MOON PHASE** ○

My "I am" Affirmation of the day: _____

Today I am grateful for: _____

I am manifesting: _____

☐ I visualized my dream coming true for 2–5 minutes.   ☐ I realized what no longer serves me & imagined my problems healed.   ☐ I made time for self-care today.

FRIDAY: _____ / _____   **MOOD:** _____   **MOON PHASE** ○

My "I am" Affirmation of the day: _____

Today I am grateful for: _____

I am manifesting: _____

☐ I visualized my dream coming true for 2–5 minutes.   ☐ I realized what no longer serves me & imagined my problems healed.   ☐ I made time for self-care today.

SATURDAY: _____ / _____   **MOOD:** _____   **MOON PHASE** ○

My "I am" Affirmation of the day: _____

Today I am grateful for: _____

I am manifesting: _____

☐ I visualized my dream coming true for 2–5 minutes.   ☐ I realized what no longer serves me & imagined my problems healed.   ☐ I made time for self-care today.

SUNDAY: _____ / _____   **MOOD:** _____   **MOON PHASE** ○

My "I am" Affirmation of the day: _____

Today I am grateful for: _____

I am manifesting: _____

☐ I visualized my dream coming true for 2–5 minutes.   ☐ I realized what no longer serves me & imagined my problems healed.   ☐ I made time for self-care today.

THE BEST THING THAT HAPPENED TO ME THIS WEEK WAS:

week 35

Your feelings construct your manifestations. Create some good feelings by writing about the happiest days of your life. As you write them down, take a moment to really feel all the emotions you felt those days. This will help you attract more amazing days and will cultivate gratitude for past experiences.

_____

_____

_____

MONDAY: _____ / _____   MOOD: _____   MOON PHASE ◯

My "I am" Affirmation of the day: _____

Today I am grateful for: _____

_____

I am manifesting: _____

| | I visualized my dream coming true for 2-5 minutes. | | I realized what no longer serves me & imagined my problems healed. | | I made time for self-care today. |

TUESDAY: _____ / _____   MOOD: _____   MOON PHASE ◯

My "I am" Affirmation of the day: _____

Today I am grateful for: _____

_____

I am manifesting: _____

| | I visualized my dream coming true for 2-5 minutes. | | I realized what no longer serves me & imagined my problems healed. | | I made time for self-care today. |

WEDNESDAY: _____ / _____   MOOD: _____   MOON PHASE ◯

My "I am" Affirmation of the day: _____

Today I am grateful for: _____

_____

I am manifesting: _____

| | I visualized my dream coming true for 2-5 minutes. | | I realized what no longer serves me & imagined my problems healed. | | I made time for self-care today. |

"Instead of trying to make your life perfect, give yourself the freedom to make it an adventure, and go ever upward." —Drew Houston

THURSDAY: _____/_____   MOOD: _____   MOON PHASE ◯

My "I am" Affirmation of the day: _____
Today I am grateful for: _____
_____

I am manifesting: _____

☐ I visualized my dream   ☐ I realized what no longer serves me   ☐ I made time for
  coming true for 2-5 minutes.   & imagined my problems healed.   self-care today.

FRIDAY: _____/_____   MOOD: _____   MOON PHASE ◯

My "I am" Affirmation of the day: _____
Today I am grateful for: _____
_____

I am manifesting: _____

☐ I visualized my dream   ☐ I realized what no longer serves me   ☐ I made time for
  coming true for 2-5 minutes.   & imagined my problems healed.   self-care today.

SATURDAY: _____/_____   MOOD: _____   MOON PHASE ◯

My "I am" Affirmation of the day: _____
Today I am grateful for: _____
_____

I am manifesting: _____

☐ I visualized my dream   ☐ I realized what no longer serves me   ☐ I made time for
  coming true for 2-5 minutes.   & imagined my problems healed.   self-care today.

SUNDAY: _____/_____   MOOD: _____   MOON PHASE ◯

My "I am" Affirmation of the day: _____
Today I am grateful for: _____
_____

I am manifesting: _____

☐ I visualized my dream   ☐ I realized what no longer serves me   ☐ I made time for
  coming true for 2-5 minutes.   & imagined my problems healed.   self-care today.

THE BEST THING THAT HAPPENED TO ME THIS WEEK WAS:

week 36

Gratitude Spree: List everything you are grateful for. Start small with things like your fingertips, your bed, your eyesight, and build to larger things like your best friend and every cent you have in the bank.

_____

_____

_____

MOnDaY: ____/____   MOOD: _____   MOOn PHase ○

My "I am" Affirmation of the day: _____

Today I am grateful for: _____

_____

I am manifesting: _____

☐ I visualized my dream coming true for 2-5 minutes.   ☐ I realized what no longer serves me & imagined my problems healed.   ☐ I made time for self-care today.

TUESDaY: ____/____   MOOD: _____   MOOn PHase ○

My "I am" Affirmation of the day: _____

Today I am grateful for: _____

_____

I am manifesting: _____

☐ I visualized my dream coming true for 2-5 minutes.   ☐ I realized what no longer serves me & imagined my problems healed.   ☐ I made time for self-care today.

WeDnesDaY: ____/____   MOOD: _____   MOOn PHase ○

My "I am" Affirmation of the day: _____

Today I am grateful for: _____

_____

I am manifesting: _____

☐ I visualized my dream coming true for 2-5 minutes.   ☐ I realized what no longer serves me & imagined my problems healed.   ☐ I made time for self-care today.

THURSDAY: _____ / _____   MOOD: _____   MOON PHASE ⚪

My "I am" Affirmation of the day: _____
Today I am grateful for: _____

I am manifesting: _____

☐ I visualized my dream   ☐ I realized what no longer serves me   ☐ I made time for
  coming true for 2-5 minutes.   & imagined my problems healed.   self-care today.

FRIDAY: _____ / _____   MOOD: _____   MOON PHASE ⚪

My "I am" Affirmation of the day: _____
Today I am grateful for: _____

I am manifesting: _____

☐ I visualized my dream   ☐ I realized what no longer serves me   ☐ I made time for
  coming true for 2-5 minutes.   & imagined my problems healed.   self-care today.

SATURDAY: _____ / _____   MOOD: _____   MOON PHASE ⚪

My "I am" Affirmation of the day: _____
Today I am grateful for: _____

I am manifesting: _____

☐ I visualized my dream   ☐ I realized what no longer serves me   ☐ I made time for
  coming true for 2-5 minutes.   & imagined my problems healed.   self-care today.

SUNDAY: _____ / _____   MOOD: _____   MOON PHASE ⚪

My "I am" Affirmation of the day: _____
Today I am grateful for: _____

I am manifesting: _____

☐ I visualized my dream   ☐ I realized what no longer serves me   ☐ I made time for
  coming true for 2-5 minutes.   & imagined my problems healed.   self-care today.

THE BEST THING THAT HAPPENED TO ME THIS WEEK WAS:

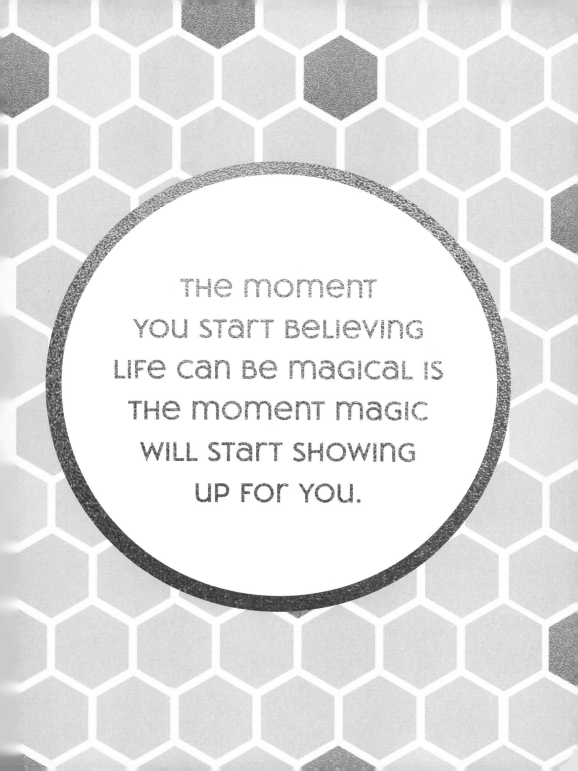

THE MOMENT
YOU START BELIEVING
LIFE CAN BE MAGICAL IS
THE MOMENT MAGIC
WILL START SHOWING
UP FOR YOU.

OPEN YOUR EYES AND ACTIVELY CHOOSE
TO SEE THE MAGIC IN YOUR EVERYDAY LIFE.
BEAUTIFUL SUNSETS, FLOWERS AND BUTTERFLIES,
THE STARS AND THE MOON, KINDNESS AMONGST
STRANGERS, THINGS JUST HAPPENING TO
WORK OUT, BIRTHDAYS, AND TRUE LOVE ARE
ABSOLUTELY ALL FORMS OF MAGIC.

What things in your life feel magical to you?

week 37

If money were not an issue, you knew you couldn't fail, and all your dreams came true, what would your ideal life be like? Write in the present tense as if you are already living it. Get as detailed as possible to help you gain clarity.

_____

_____

_____

MONDAY: _____ / _____   **MOOD:** _____   **MOON PHASE** ⚪

My "I am" Affirmation of the day: _____

Today I am grateful for: _____

I am manifesting: _____

☐ I visualized my dream coming true for 2-5 minutes.   ☐ I realized what no longer serves me & imagined my problems healed.   ☐ I made time for self-care today.

TUESDAY: _____ / _____   **MOOD:** _____   **MOON PHASE** ⚪

My "I am" Affirmation of the day: _____

Today I am grateful for: _____

I am manifesting: _____

☐ I visualized my dream coming true for 2-5 minutes.   ☐ I realized what no longer serves me & imagined my problems healed.   ☐ I made time for self-care today.

WEDNESDAY: _____ / _____   **MOOD:** _____   **MOON PHASE** ⚪

My "I am" Affirmation of the day: _____

Today I am grateful for: _____

I am manifesting: _____

☐ I visualized my dream coming true for 2-5 minutes.   ☐ I realized what no longer serves me & imagined my problems healed.   ☐ I made time for self-care today.

"No one can make you feel inferior without your consent." —Rosa Parks

THURSDAY: _____ / _____   **MOOD:** _____   **MOON PHASE** ◯

My "I am" Affirmation of the day: _____

Today I am grateful for: _____

_____

I am manifesting: _____

_____

☐ I visualized my dream coming true for 2-5 minutes.   ☐ I realized what no longer serves me & imagined my problems healed.   ☐ I made time for self-care today.

FRIDAY: _____ / _____   **MOOD:** _____   **MOON PHASE** ◯

My "I am" Affirmation of the day: _____

Today I am grateful for: _____

_____

I am manifesting: _____

_____

☐ I visualized my dream coming true for 2-5 minutes.   ☐ I realized what no longer serves me & imagined my problems healed.   ☐ I made time for self-care today.

SATURDAY: _____ / _____   **MOOD:** _____   **MOON PHASE** ◯

My "I am" Affirmation of the day: _____

Today I am grateful for: _____

_____

I am manifesting: _____

_____

☐ I visualized my dream coming true for 2-5 minutes.   ☐ I realized what no longer serves me & imagined my problems healed.   ☐ I made time for self-care today.

SUNDAY: _____ / _____   **MOOD:** _____   **MOON PHASE** ◯

My "I am" Affirmation of the day: _____

Today I am grateful for: _____

_____

I am manifesting: _____

_____

☐ I visualized my dream coming true for 2-5 minutes.   ☐ I realized what no longer serves me & imagined my problems healed.   ☐ I made time for self-care today.

THE BEST THING THAT HAPPENED TO ME THIS WEEK WAS:

week 38

It's always great to give yourself space to deeply heal and let go, so it's time to release everything that's bothering you. Write down anything that's currently bringing you down, no matter how small, and then imagine letting it all go. After that, write about the things that you love in your life. Focus on the things that make you smile and make your heart happy.

_____

_____

_____

MONDAY: _____ / _____   **MOOD:** _____   **MOON PHASE** ⚪

My "I am" Affirmation of the day: _____

Today I am grateful for: _____

I am manifesting: _____

☐ I visualized my dream coming true for 2-5 minutes.   ☐ I realized what no longer serves me & imagined my problems healed.   ☐ I made time for self-care today.

TUESDAY: _____ / _____   **MOOD:** _____   **MOON PHASE** ⚪

My "I am" Affirmation of the day: _____

Today I am grateful for: _____

I am manifesting: _____

☐ I visualized my dream coming true for 2-5 minutes.   ☐ I realized what no longer serves me & imagined my problems healed.   ☐ I made time for self-care today.

WEDNESDAY: _____ / _____   **MOOD:** _____   **MOON PHASE** ⚪

My "I am" Affirmation of the day: _____

Today I am grateful for: _____

I am manifesting: _____

☐ I visualized my dream coming true for 2-5 minutes.   ☐ I realized what no longer serves me & imagined my problems healed.   ☐ I made time for self-care today.

THURSDAY: _____ / _____   **MOOD:** _____   **MOON PHASE** ◯

My "I am" Affirmation of the day: _____

Today I am grateful for: _____

I am manifesting: _____

☐ I visualized my dream coming true for 2-5 minutes.   ☐ I realized what no longer serves me & imagined my problems healed.   ☐ I made time for self-care today.

FRIDAY: _____ / _____   **MOOD:** _____   **MOON PHASE** ◯

My "I am" Affirmation of the day: _____

Today I am grateful for: _____

I am manifesting: _____

☐ I visualized my dream coming true for 2-5 minutes.   ☐ I realized what no longer serves me & imagined my problems healed.   ☐ I made time for self-care today.

SATURDAY: _____ / _____   **MOOD:** _____   **MOON PHASE** ◯

My "I am" Affirmation of the day: _____

Today I am grateful for: _____

I am manifesting: _____

☐ I visualized my dream coming true for 2-5 minutes.   ☐ I realized what no longer serves me & imagined my problems healed.   ☐ I made time for self-care today.

SUNDAY: _____ / _____   **MOOD:** _____   **MOON PHASE** ◯

My "I am" Affirmation of the day: _____

Today I am grateful for: _____

I am manifesting: _____

☐ I visualized my dream coming true for 2-5 minutes.   ☐ I realized what no longer serves me & imagined my problems healed.   ☐ I made time for self-care today.

THE BEST THING THAT HAPPENED TO ME THIS WEEK WAS:

week 39

A fairy godmother is granting you three wishes. What would they be? She's also letting you grant one wish to everyone you love. What would they be? After each, take a moment to really envision it happening for yourself and the others.

_____

_____

_____

monday: _____ / _____   mood: _____   moon phase ⬤

My "I am" Affirmation of the day: _____

Today I am grateful for: _____

I am manifesting: _____

☐ I visualized my dream coming true for 2–5 minutes. ☐ I realized what no longer serves me & imagined my problems healed. ☐ I made time for self-care today.

tuesday: _____ / _____   mood: _____   moon phase ⬤

My "I am" Affirmation of the day: _____

Today I am grateful for: _____

I am manifesting: _____

☐ I visualized my dream coming true for 2–5 minutes. ☐ I realized what no longer serves me & imagined my problems healed. ☐ I made time for self-care today.

wednesday: _____ / _____   mood: _____   moon phase ⬤

My "I am" Affirmation of the day: _____

Today I am grateful for: _____

I am manifesting: _____

☐ I visualized my dream coming true for 2–5 minutes. ☐ I realized what no longer serves me & imagined my problems healed. ☐ I made time for self-care today.

"We are still masters of our fate. We are still captains of our souls." —Winston Churchill

THURSDAY: _____ / _____   **MOOD:** _____   **MOON PHASE** ◯

My "I am" Affirmation of the day: _____

Today I am grateful for: _____

_____

I am manifesting: _____

_____

☐ I visualized my dream coming true for 2-5 minutes.   ☐ I realized what no longer serves me & imagined my problems healed.   ☐ I made time for self-care today.

FRIDAY: _____ / _____   **MOOD:** _____   **MOON PHASE** ◯

My "I am" Affirmation of the day: _____

Today I am grateful for: _____

_____

I am manifesting: _____

_____

☐ I visualized my dream coming true for 2-5 minutes.   ☐ I realized what no longer serves me & imagined my problems healed.   ☐ I made time for self-care today.

SATURDAY: _____ / _____   **MOOD:** _____   **MOON PHASE** ◯

My "I am" Affirmation of the day: _____

Today I am grateful for: _____

_____

I am manifesting: _____

_____

☐ I visualized my dream coming true for 2-5 minutes.   ☐ I realized what no longer serves me & imagined my problems healed.   ☐ I made time for self-care today.

SUNDAY: _____ / _____   **MOOD:** _____   **MOON PHASE** ◯

My "I am" Affirmation of the day: _____

Today I am grateful for: _____

_____

I am manifesting: _____

_____

☐ I visualized my dream coming true for 2-5 minutes.   ☐ I realized what no longer serves me & imagined my problems healed.   ☐ I made time for self-care today.

THE BEST THING THAT HAPPENED TO ME THIS WEEK WAS:

week 40

See the true beauty in yourself. Write what you appreciate about yourself—both your external appearance and your personality.

_____

_____

_____

MONDAY: _____ / _____   MOOD: _____   MOON PHASE ◯

My "I am" Affirmation of the day: _____

Today I am grateful for: _____

_____

I am manifesting: _____

| ☐ I visualized my dream coming true for 2-5 minutes. | ☐ I realized what no longer serves me & imagined my problems healed. | ☐ I made time for self-care today. |

TUESDAY: _____ / _____   MOOD: _____   MOON PHASE ◯

My "I am" Affirmation of the day: _____

Today I am grateful for: _____

_____

I am manifesting: _____

| ☐ I visualized my dream coming true for 2-5 minutes. | ☐ I realized what no longer serves me & imagined my problems healed. | ☐ I made time for self-care today. |

WEDNESDAY: _____ / _____   MOOD: _____   MOON PHASE ◯

My "I am" Affirmation of the day: _____

Today I am grateful for: _____

_____

I am manifesting: _____

| ☐ I visualized my dream coming true for 2-5 minutes. | ☐ I realized what no longer serves me & imagined my problems healed. | ☐ I made time for self-care today. |

THURSDAY: _____ / _____   **MOOD:** _____   **MOON PHASE** ◯

My "I am" Affirmation of the day: _____

Today I am grateful for: _____

I am manifesting: _____

☐ I visualized my dream coming true for 2-5 minutes.   ☐ I realized what no longer serves me & imagined my problems healed.   ☐ I made time for self-care today.

FRIDAY: _____ / _____   **MOOD:** _____   **MOON PHASE** ◯

My "I am" Affirmation of the day: _____

Today I am grateful for: _____

I am manifesting: _____

☐ I visualized my dream coming true for 2-5 minutes.   ☐ I realized what no longer serves me & imagined my problems healed.   ☐ I made time for self-care today.

SATURDAY: _____ / _____   **MOOD:** _____   **MOON PHASE** ◯

My "I am" Affirmation of the day: _____

Today I am grateful for: _____

I am manifesting: _____

☐ I visualized my dream coming true for 2-5 minutes.   ☐ I realized what no longer serves me & imagined my problems healed.   ☐ I made time for self-care today.

SUNDAY: _____ / _____   **MOOD:** _____   **MOON PHASE** ◯

My "I am" Affirmation of the day: _____

Today I am grateful for: _____

I am manifesting: _____

☐ I visualized my dream coming true for 2-5 minutes.   ☐ I realized what no longer serves me & imagined my problems healed.   ☐ I made time for self-care today.

THE BEST THING THAT HAPPENED TO ME THIS WEEK WAS:

week 41

Your feelings construct your manifestations. Create some good feelings by writing about the happiest days of your life. As you write them down, take a moment to really feel all the emotions you felt those days. This will help you attract more amazing days and will cultivate gratitude for past experiences.

_____

_____

_____

MONDAY: ____/____ **MOOD:** _____ **MOON PHASE** ◯

My "I am" Affirmation of the day: _____

Today I am grateful for: _____

I am manifesting: _____

☐ I visualized my dream coming true for 2-5 minutes.
☐ I realized what no longer serves me & imagined my problems healed.
☐ I made time for self-care today.

TUESDAY: ____/____ **MOOD:** _____ **MOON PHASE** ◯

My "I am" Affirmation of the day: _____

Today I am grateful for: _____

I am manifesting: _____

☐ I visualized my dream coming true for 2-5 minutes.
☐ I realized what no longer serves me & imagined my problems healed.
☐ I made time for self-care today.

WEDNESDAY: ____/____ **MOOD:** _____ **MOON PHASE** ◯

My "I am" Affirmation of the day: _____

Today I am grateful for: _____

I am manifesting: _____

☐ I visualized my dream coming true for 2-5 minutes.
☐ I realized what no longer serves me & imagined my problems healed.
☐ I made time for self-care today.

"The best way to predict the future is to create it." —Abraham Lincoln

THURSDAY: _____ / _____   **MOOD:** _____   **MOON PHASE** ◯

My "I am" Affirmation of the day: _____

Today I am grateful for: _____

_____

I am manifesting: _____

_____

☐ I visualized my dream coming true for 2-5 minutes.   ☐ I realized what no longer serves me & imagined my problems healed.   ☐ I made time for self-care today.

FRIDAY: _____ / _____   **MOOD:** _____   **MOON PHASE** ◯

My "I am" Affirmation of the day: _____

Today I am grateful for: _____

_____

I am manifesting: _____

_____

☐ I visualized my dream coming true for 2-5 minutes.   ☐ I realized what no longer serves me & imagined my problems healed.   ☐ I made time for self-care today.

SATURDAY: _____ / _____   **MOOD:** _____   **MOON PHASE** ◯

My "I am" Affirmation of the day: _____

Today I am grateful for: _____

_____

I am manifesting: _____

_____

☐ I visualized my dream coming true for 2-5 minutes.   ☐ I realized what no longer serves me & imagined my problems healed.   ☐ I made time for self-care today.

SUNDAY: _____ / _____   **MOOD:** _____   **MOON PHASE** ◯

My "I am" Affirmation of the day: _____

Today I am grateful for: _____

_____

I am manifesting: _____

_____

☐ I visualized my dream coming true for 2-5 minutes.   ☐ I realized what no longer serves me & imagined my problems healed.   ☐ I made time for self-care today.

THE BEST THING THAT HAPPENED TO ME THIS WEEK WAS:

week 42

Gratitude Spree: List everything you are grateful for. Start small with things like your fingertips, your bed, your eyesight, and build to larger things like your best friend and every cent you have in the bank.

_____

_____

_____

MONDAY: _____ / _____   **MOOD:** _____   **MOON PHASE** ○

My "I am" Affirmation of the day: _____

Today I am grateful for: _____

I am manifesting: _____

☐ I visualized my dream coming true for 2-5 minutes.   ☐ I realized what no longer serves me & imagined my problems healed.   ☐ I made time for self-care today.

TUESDAY: _____ / _____   **MOOD:** _____   **MOON PHASE** ○

My "I am" Affirmation of the day: _____

Today I am grateful for: _____

I am manifesting: _____

☐ I visualized my dream coming true for 2-5 minutes.   ☐ I realized what no longer serves me & imagined my problems healed.   ☐ I made time for self-care today.

WEDNESDAY: _____ / _____   **MOOD:** _____   **MOON PHASE** ○

My "I am" Affirmation of the day: _____

Today I am grateful for: _____

I am manifesting: _____

☐ I visualized my dream coming true for 2-5 minutes.   ☐ I realized what no longer serves me & imagined my problems healed.   ☐ I made time for self-care today.

THURSDAY: _____ / _____   **MOOD:** _____   **MOON PHASE** ◯

My "I am" Affirmation of the day: _____

Today I am grateful for: _____

I am manifesting: _____

☐ I visualized my dream coming true for 2-5 minutes.   ☐ I realized what no longer serves me & imagined my problems healed.   ☐ I made time for self-care today.

FRIDAY: _____ / _____   **MOOD:** _____   **MOON PHASE** ◯

My "I am" Affirmation of the day: _____

Today I am grateful for: _____

I am manifesting: _____

☐ I visualized my dream coming true for 2-5 minutes.   ☐ I realized what no longer serves me & imagined my problems healed.   ☐ I made time for self-care today.

SATURDAY: _____ / _____   **MOOD:** _____   **MOON PHASE** ◯

My "I am" Affirmation of the day: _____

Today I am grateful for: _____

I am manifesting: _____

☐ I visualized my dream coming true for 2-5 minutes.   ☐ I realized what no longer serves me & imagined my problems healed.   ☐ I made time for self-care today.

SUNDAY: _____ / _____   **MOOD:** _____   **MOON PHASE** ◯

My "I am" Affirmation of the day: _____

Today I am grateful for: _____

I am manifesting: _____

☐ I visualized my dream coming true for 2-5 minutes.   ☐ I realized what no longer serves me & imagined my problems healed.   ☐ I made time for self-care today.

THE BEST THING THAT HAPPENED TO ME THIS WEEK WAS:

YOU
Deserve
TO
HeaL

Forgiveness is such an important practice that really sets you free. The Hawaiian culture has a great forgiveness practice called Ho'oponopono. It's a prayer in which you imagine the person you need to forgive and say: "I am sorry. Please forgive me, I forgive you. I thank you. I love you." Repeat it as many times as you feel the need to and while doing so, imagine both yourself and the other person surrounded in beautiful light. Imagine the situation completely healed. Imagine yourself free.

Who do you need to forgive?

week 43

If money were not an issue, you knew you couldn't fail, and all your dreams came true, what would your ideal life be like? Write in the present tense as if you are already living it. Get as detailed as possible to help you gain clarity.

_____

_____

_____

MONDAY: _____ / _____   MOOD: _____   MOON PHASE ⚪

My "I am" Affirmation of the day: _____

Today I am grateful for: _____

I am manifesting: _____

- [ ] I visualized my dream coming true for 2-5 minutes.
- [ ] I realized what no longer serves me & imagined my problems healed.
- [ ] I made time for self-care today.

TUESDAY: _____ / _____   MOOD: _____   MOON PHASE ⚪

My "I am" Affirmation of the day: _____

Today I am grateful for: _____

I am manifesting: _____

- [ ] I visualized my dream coming true for 2-5 minutes.
- [ ] I realized what no longer serves me & imagined my problems healed.
- [ ] I made time for self-care today.

WEDNESDAY: _____ / _____   MOOD: _____   MOON PHASE ⚪

My "I am" Affirmation of the day: _____

Today I am grateful for: _____

I am manifesting: _____

- [ ] I visualized my dream coming true for 2-5 minutes.
- [ ] I realized what no longer serves me & imagined my problems healed.
- [ ] I made time for self-care today.

"Happiness is not a state to arrive at, but a manner of traveling." —Margaret Lee Runbeck

THURSDAY: _____ / _____   **MOOD:** _____   **MOON PHASE** ◯

My "I am" Affirmation of the day: _____

Today I am grateful for: _____

I am manifesting: _____

☐ I visualized my dream coming true for 2-5 minutes.   ☐ I realized what no longer serves me & imagined my problems healed.   ☐ I made time for self-care today.

FRIDAY: _____ / _____   **MOOD:** _____   **MOON PHASE** ◯

My "I am" Affirmation of the day: _____

Today I am grateful for: _____

I am manifesting: _____

☐ I visualized my dream coming true for 2-5 minutes.   ☐ I realized what no longer serves me & imagined my problems healed.   ☐ I made time for self-care today.

SATURDAY: _____ / _____   **MOOD:** _____   **MOON PHASE** ◯

My "I am" Affirmation of the day: _____

Today I am grateful for: _____

I am manifesting: _____

☐ I visualized my dream coming true for 2-5 minutes.   ☐ I realized what no longer serves me & imagined my problems healed.   ☐ I made time for self-care today.

SUNDAY: _____ / _____   **MOOD:** _____   **MOON PHASE** ◯

My "I am" Affirmation of the day: _____

Today I am grateful for: _____

I am manifesting: _____

☐ I visualized my dream coming true for 2-5 minutes.   ☐ I realized what no longer serves me & imagined my problems healed.   ☐ I made time for self-care today.

THE BEST THING THAT HAPPENED TO ME THIS WEEK WAS:

week 44

It's always great to give yourself space to deeply heal and let go, so it's time to release everything that's bothering you. Write down anything that's currently bringing you down, no matter how small, and then imagine letting it all go. After that, write about the things that you love in your life. Focus on the things that make you smile and make your heart happy.

_____

_____

_____

MONDAY: _____ / _____   MOOD: _____   MOON PHASE ◯

My "I am" Affirmation of the day: _____

Today I am grateful for: _____

I am manifesting: _____

☐ I visualized my dream coming true for 2-5 minutes.   ☐ I realized what no longer serves me & imagined my problems healed.   ☐ I made time for self-care today.

TUESDAY: _____ / _____   MOOD: _____   MOON PHASE ◯

My "I am" Affirmation of the day: _____

Today I am grateful for: _____

I am manifesting: _____

☐ I visualized my dream coming true for 2-5 minutes.   ☐ I realized what no longer serves me & imagined my problems healed.   ☐ I made time for self-care today.

WEDNESDAY: _____ / _____   MOOD: _____   MOON PHASE ◯

My "I am" Affirmation of the day: _____

Today I am grateful for: _____

I am manifesting: _____

☐ I visualized my dream coming true for 2-5 minutes.   ☐ I realized what no longer serves me & imagined my problems healed.   ☐ I made time for self-care today.

THURSDAY: _____ / _____   **MOOD:** _____   **MOON PHASE** ⚪

My "I am" Affirmation of the day: _____

Today I am grateful for: _____

I am manifesting: _____

☐ I visualized my dream coming true for 2-5 minutes.   ☐ I realized what no longer serves me & imagined my problems healed.   ☐ I made time for self-care today.

FRIDAY: _____ / _____   **MOOD:** _____   **MOON PHASE** ⚪

My "I am" Affirmation of the day: _____

Today I am grateful for: _____

I am manifesting: _____

☐ I visualized my dream coming true for 2-5 minutes.   ☐ I realized what no longer serves me & imagined my problems healed.   ☐ I made time for self-care today.

SATURDAY: _____ / _____   **MOOD:** _____   **MOON PHASE** ⚪

My "I am" Affirmation of the day: _____

Today I am grateful for: _____

I am manifesting: _____

☐ I visualized my dream coming true for 2-5 minutes.   ☐ I realized what no longer serves me & imagined my problems healed.   ☐ I made time for self-care today.

SUNDAY: _____ / _____   **MOOD:** _____   **MOON PHASE** ⚪

My "I am" Affirmation of the day: _____

Today I am grateful for: _____

I am manifesting: _____

☐ I visualized my dream coming true for 2-5 minutes.   ☐ I realized what no longer serves me & imagined my problems healed.   ☐ I made time for self-care today.

THE BEST THING THAT HAPPENED TO ME THIS WEEK WAS:

week 45

A fairy godmother is granting you three wishes. What would they be? She's also letting you grant one wish to everyone you love. What would they be? After each, take a moment to really envision it happening for yourself and the others.

_____

_____

_____

MONDAY: _____ / _____   **MOOD:** _____   **MOON PHASE** ○

My "I am" Affirmation of the day: _____

Today I am grateful for: _____

I am manifesting: _____

☐ I visualized my dream coming true for 2-5 minutes. ☐ I realized what no longer serves me & imagined my problems healed. ☐ I made time for self-care today.

TUESDAY: _____ / _____   **MOOD:** _____   **MOON PHASE** ○

My "I am" Affirmation of the day: _____

Today I am grateful for: _____

I am manifesting: _____

☐ I visualized my dream coming true for 2-5 minutes. ☐ I realized what no longer serves me & imagined my problems healed. ☐ I made time for self-care today.

WEDNESDAY: _____ / _____   **MOOD:** _____   **MOON PHASE** ○

My "I am" Affirmation of the day: _____

Today I am grateful for: _____

I am manifesting: _____

☐ I visualized my dream coming true for 2-5 minutes. ☐ I realized what no longer serves me & imagined my problems healed. ☐ I made time for self-care today.

"Let yourself be drawn by the stronger pull of that which you truly love." —Rumi

THURSDAY: _____ / _____   **MOOD:** _____   **MOON PHASE** ○

My "I am" Affirmation of the day: _____

Today I am grateful for: _____

I am manifesting: _____

☐ I visualized my dream coming true for 2-5 minutes.   ☐ I realized what no longer serves me & imagined my problems healed.   ☐ I made time for self-care today.

FRIDAY: _____ / _____   **MOOD:** _____   **MOON PHASE** ○

My "I am" Affirmation of the day: _____

Today I am grateful for: _____

I am manifesting: _____

☐ I visualized my dream coming true for 2-5 minutes.   ☐ I realized what no longer serves me & imagined my problems healed.   ☐ I made time for self-care today.

SATURDAY: _____ / _____   **MOOD:** _____   **MOON PHASE** ○

My "I am" Affirmation of the day: _____

Today I am grateful for: _____

I am manifesting: _____

☐ I visualized my dream coming true for 2-5 minutes.   ☐ I realized what no longer serves me & imagined my problems healed.   ☐ I made time for self-care today.

SUNDAY: _____ / _____   **MOOD:** _____   **MOON PHASE** ○

My "I am" Affirmation of the day: _____

Today I am grateful for: _____

I am manifesting: _____

☐ I visualized my dream coming true for 2-5 minutes.   ☐ I realized what no longer serves me & imagined my problems healed.   ☐ I made time for self-care today.

THE BEST THING THAT HAPPENED TO ME THIS WEEK WAS:

week 46

See the true beauty in yourself. Write what you appreciate about yourself—both your external appearance and your personality.

_____

_____

_____

MONDAY: _____ / _____   **MOOD:** _____   **MOON PHASE** ◯

My "I am" Affirmation of the day: _____

Today I am grateful for: _____

I am manifesting: _____

☐ I visualized my dream coming true for 2-5 minutes.   ☐ I realized what no longer serves me & imagined my problems healed.   ☐ I made time for self-care today.

TUESDAY: _____ / _____   **MOOD:** _____   **MOON PHASE** ◯

My "I am" Affirmation of the day: _____

Today I am grateful for: _____

I am manifesting: _____

☐ I visualized my dream coming true for 2-5 minutes.   ☐ I realized what no longer serves me & imagined my problems healed.   ☐ I made time for self-care today.

WEDNESDAY: _____ / _____   **MOOD:** _____   **MOON PHASE** ◯

My "I am" Affirmation of the day: _____

Today I am grateful for: _____

I am manifesting: _____

☐ I visualized my dream coming true for 2-5 minutes.   ☐ I realized what no longer serves me & imagined my problems healed.   ☐ I made time for self-care today.

THURSDAY: _____ / _____ MOOD: _____ MOON PHASE ○

My "I am" Affirmation of the day: _____

Today I am grateful for: _____

_____

I am manifesting: _____

_____

☐ I visualized my dream coming true for 2-5 minutes.　☐ I realized what no longer serves me & imagined my problems healed.　☐ I made time for self-care today.

FRIDAY: _____ / _____ MOOD: _____ MOON PHASE ○

My "I am" Affirmation of the day: _____

Today I am grateful for: _____

_____

I am manifesting: _____

_____

☐ I visualized my dream coming true for 2-5 minutes.　☐ I realized what no longer serves me & imagined my problems healed.　☐ I made time for self-care today.

SATURDAY: _____ / _____ MOOD: _____ MOON PHASE ○

My "I am" Affirmation of the day: _____

Today I am grateful for: _____

_____

I am manifesting: _____

_____

☐ I visualized my dream coming true for 2-5 minutes.　☐ I realized what no longer serves me & imagined my problems healed.　☐ I made time for self-care today.

SUNDAY: _____ / _____ MOOD: _____ MOON PHASE ○

My "I am" Affirmation of the day: _____

Today I am grateful for: _____

_____

I am manifesting: _____

_____

☐ I visualized my dream coming true for 2-5 minutes.　☐ I realized what no longer serves me & imagined my problems healed.　☐ I made time for self-care today.

THE BEST THING THAT HAPPENED TO ME THIS WEEK WAS:

week 47

Your feelings construct your manifestations. Create some good feelings by writing about the happiest days of your life. As you write them down, take a moment to really feel all the emotions you felt those days. This will help you attract more amazing days and will cultivate gratitude for past experiences.

_____

_____

_____

MONDAY: _____ / _____   **MOOD:** _____   **MOON PHASE** ◯

My "I am" Affirmation of the day: _____

Today I am grateful for: _____

_____

I am manifesting: _____

- [ ] I visualized my dream coming true for 2-5 minutes.
- [ ] I realized what no longer serves me & imagined my problems healed.
- [ ] I made time for self-care today.

TUESDAY: _____ / _____   **MOOD:** _____   **MOON PHASE** ◯

My "I am" Affirmation of the day: _____

Today I am grateful for: _____

_____

I am manifesting: _____

- [ ] I visualized my dream coming true for 2-5 minutes.
- [ ] I realized what no longer serves me & imagined my problems healed.
- [ ] I made time for self-care today.

WEDNESDAY: _____ / _____   **MOOD:** _____   **MOON PHASE** ◯

My "I am" Affirmation of the day: _____

Today I am grateful for: _____

_____

I am manifesting: _____

- [ ] I visualized my dream coming true for 2-5 minutes.
- [ ] I realized what no longer serves me & imagined my problems healed.
- [ ] I made time for self-care today.

"What would life be if we had no courage to attempt anything?" —Vincent Van Gogh

THURSDAY: _____ / _____ MOOD: _____ MOON PHASE ⚪

My "I am" Affirmation of the day: _____

Today I am grateful for: _____

I am manifesting: _____

☐ I visualized my dream coming true for 2-5 minutes. ☐ I realized what no longer serves me & imagined my problems healed. ☐ I made time for self-care today.

FRIDAY: _____ / _____ MOOD: _____ MOON PHASE ⚪

My "I am" Affirmation of the day: _____

Today I am grateful for: _____

I am manifesting: _____

☐ I visualized my dream coming true for 2-5 minutes. ☐ I realized what no longer serves me & imagined my problems healed. ☐ I made time for self-care today.

SATURDAY: _____ / _____ MOOD: _____ MOON PHASE ⚪

My "I am" Affirmation of the day: _____

Today I am grateful for: _____

I am manifesting: _____

☐ I visualized my dream coming true for 2-5 minutes. ☐ I realized what no longer serves me & imagined my problems healed. ☐ I made time for self-care today.

SUNDAY: _____ / _____ MOOD: _____ MOON PHASE ⚪

My "I am" Affirmation of the day: _____

Today I am grateful for: _____

I am manifesting: _____

☐ I visualized my dream coming true for 2-5 minutes. ☐ I realized what no longer serves me & imagined my problems healed. ☐ I made time for self-care today.

THE BEST THING THAT HAPPENED TO ME THIS WEEK WAS:

week 48

Gratitude Spree: List everything you are grateful for. Start small with things like your fingertips, your bed, your eyesight, and build to larger things like your best friend and every cent you have in the bank.

_____

_____

_____

MONDAY: _____ / _____   MOOD: _____   MOON PHASE ⚪

My "I am" Affirmation of the day: _____

Today I am grateful for: _____

I am manifesting: _____

☐ I visualized my dream coming true for 2-5 minutes.   ☐ I realized what no longer serves me & imagined my problems healed.   ☐ I made time for self-care today.

TUESDAY: _____ / _____   MOOD: _____   MOON PHASE ⚪

My "I am" Affirmation of the day: _____

Today I am grateful for: _____

I am manifesting: _____

☐ I visualized my dream coming true for 2-5 minutes.   ☐ I realized what no longer serves me & imagined my problems healed.   ☐ I made time for self-care today.

WEDNESDAY: _____ / _____   MOOD: _____   MOON PHASE ⚪

My "I am" Affirmation of the day: _____

Today I am grateful for: _____

I am manifesting: _____

☐ I visualized my dream coming true for 2-5 minutes.   ☐ I realized what no longer serves me & imagined my problems healed.   ☐ I made time for self-care today.

THURSDAY: ____ / ____   **MOOD:** _____   **MOON PHASE** ⃝

My "I am" Affirmation of the day: _____

Today I am grateful for: _____

I am manifesting: _____

☐ I visualized my dream coming true for 2-5 minutes.   ☐ I realized what no longer serves me & imagined my problems healed.   ☐ I made time for self-care today.

FRIDAY: ____ / ____   **MOOD:** _____   **MOON PHASE** ⃝

My "I am" Affirmation of the day: _____

Today I am grateful for: _____

I am manifesting: _____

☐ I visualized my dream coming true for 2-5 minutes.   ☐ I realized what no longer serves me & imagined my problems healed.   ☐ I made time for self-care today.

SATURDAY: ____ / ____   **MOOD:** _____   **MOON PHASE** ⃝

My "I am" Affirmation of the day: _____

Today I am grateful for: _____

I am manifesting: _____

☐ I visualized my dream coming true for 2-5 minutes.   ☐ I realized what no longer serves me & imagined my problems healed.   ☐ I made time for self-care today.

SUNDAY: ____ / ____   **MOOD:** _____   **MOON PHASE** ⃝

My "I am" Affirmation of the day: _____

Today I am grateful for: _____

I am manifesting: _____

☐ I visualized my dream coming true for 2-5 minutes.   ☐ I realized what no longer serves me & imagined my problems healed.   ☐ I made time for self-care today.

THE BEST THING THAT HAPPENED TO ME THIS WEEK WAS:

week 49

If money were not an issue, you knew you couldn't fail, and all your dreams came true, what would your ideal life be like? Write in the present tense as if you are already living it. Get as detailed as possible to help you gain clarity.

_____

_____

_____

MONDAY: _____ / _____   MOOD: _____   MOON PHASE ○

My "I am" Affirmation of the day: _____

Today I am grateful for: _____

I am manifesting: _____

- [ ] I visualized my dream coming true for 2-5 minutes.
- [ ] I realized what no longer serves me & imagined my problems healed.
- [ ] I made time for self-care today.

TUESDAY: _____ / _____   MOOD: _____   MOON PHASE ○

My "I am" Affirmation of the day: _____

Today I am grateful for: _____

I am manifesting: _____

- [ ] I visualized my dream coming true for 2-5 minutes.
- [ ] I realized what no longer serves me & imagined my problems healed.
- [ ] I made time for self-care today.

WEDNESDAY: _____ / _____   MOOD: _____   MOON PHASE ○

My "I am" Affirmation of the day: _____

Today I am grateful for: _____

I am manifesting: _____

- [ ] I visualized my dream coming true for 2-5 minutes.
- [ ] I realized what no longer serves me & imagined my problems healed.
- [ ] I made time for self-care today.

"To be beautiful means to be yourself. You don't need to be accepted by others. You need to accept yourself." —Thich Nhat Hanh

THURSDAY: _____ / _____ **MOOD:** _____ **MOON PHASE** ⬤

My "I am" Affirmation of the day: _____

Today I am grateful for: _____

I am manifesting: _____

☐ I visualized my dream coming true for 2-5 minutes. ☐ I realized what no longer serves me & imagined my problems healed. ☐ I made time for self-care today.

FRIDAY: _____ / _____ **MOOD:** _____ **MOON PHASE** ⬤

My "I am" Affirmation of the day: _____

Today I am grateful for: _____

I am manifesting: _____

☐ I visualized my dream coming true for 2-5 minutes. ☐ I realized what no longer serves me & imagined my problems healed. ☐ I made time for self-care today.

SATURDAY: _____ / _____ **MOOD:** _____ **MOON PHASE** ⬤

My "I am" Affirmation of the day: _____

Today I am grateful for: _____

I am manifesting: _____

☐ I visualized my dream coming true for 2-5 minutes. ☐ I realized what no longer serves me & imagined my problems healed. ☐ I made time for self-care today.

SUNDAY: _____ / _____ **MOOD:** _____ **MOON PHASE** ⬤

My "I am" Affirmation of the day: _____

Today I am grateful for: _____

I am manifesting: _____

☐ I visualized my dream coming true for 2-5 minutes. ☐ I realized what no longer serves me & imagined my problems healed. ☐ I made time for self-care today.

THE BEST THING THAT HAPPENED TO ME THIS WEEK WAS:

week 50

It's always great to give yourself space to deeply heal and let go, so it's time to release everything that's bothering you. Write down anything that's currently bringing you down, no matter how small, and then imagine letting it all go. After that, write about the things that you love in your life. Focus on the things that make you smile and make your heart happy.

_____

_____

_____

MONDAY: _____ / _____   MOOD: _____   MOON PHASE ○

My "I am" Affirmation of the day: _____

Today I am grateful for: _____

I am manifesting: _____

☐ I visualized my dream coming true for 2-5 minutes.　　☐ I realized what no longer serves me & imagined my problems healed.　　☐ I made time for self-care today.

TUESDAY: _____ / _____   MOOD: _____   MOON PHASE ○

My "I am" Affirmation of the day: _____

Today I am grateful for: _____

I am manifesting: _____

☐ I visualized my dream coming true for 2-5 minutes.　　☐ I realized what no longer serves me & imagined my problems healed.　　☐ I made time for self-care today.

WEDNESDAY: _____ / _____   MOOD: _____   MOON PHASE ○

My "I am" Affirmation of the day: _____

Today I am grateful for: _____

I am manifesting: _____

☐ I visualized my dream coming true for 2-5 minutes.　　☐ I realized what no longer serves me & imagined my problems healed.　　☐ I made time for self-care today.

THursDay: _____ / _____   **mooD:** _____   **moon PHase** ◯

My "I am" Affirmation of the day: _____

Today I am grateful for: _____

I am manifesting: _____

☐   I visualized my dream   ☐   I realized what no longer serves me   ☐   I made time for
    coming true for 2-5 minutes.   & imagined my problems healed.   self-care today.

FriDay: _____ / _____   **mooD:** _____   **moon PHase** ◯

My "I am" Affirmation of the day: _____

Today I am grateful for: _____

I am manifesting: _____

☐   I visualized my dream   ☐   I realized what no longer serves me   ☐   I made time for
    coming true for 2-5 minutes.   & imagined my problems healed.   self-care today.

---

saTurDay: _____ / _____   **mooD:** _____   **moon PHase** ◯

My "I am" Affirmation of the day: _____

Today I am grateful for: _____

I am manifesting: _____

☐   I visualized my dream   ☐   I realized what no longer serves me   ☐   I made time for
    coming true for 2-5 minutes.   & imagined my problems healed.   self-care today.

---

sunDay: _____ / _____   **mooD:** _____   **moon PHase** ◯

My "I am" Affirmation of the day: _____

Today I am grateful for: _____

I am manifesting: _____

☐   I visualized my dream   ☐   I realized what no longer serves me   ☐   I made time for
    coming true for 2-5 minutes.   & imagined my problems healed.   self-care today.

THe BesT THInG THaT HaPPeneD To me THIs week was:

week 51

A fairy godmother is granting you three wishes. What would they be? She's also letting you grant one wish to everyone you love. What would they be? After each, take a moment to really envision it happening for yourself and the others.

_____

_____

_____

MONDAY: _____/_____ **MOOD:** _____ **MOON PHASE** ◯

My "I am" Affirmation of the day: _____

Today I am grateful for: _____

I am manifesting: _____

☐ I visualized my dream coming true for 2-5 minutes. ☐ I realized what no longer serves me & imagined my problems healed. ☐ I made time for self-care today.

TUESDAY: _____/_____ **MOOD:** _____ **MOON PHASE** ◯

My "I am" Affirmation of the day: _____

Today I am grateful for: _____

I am manifesting: _____

☐ I visualized my dream coming true for 2-5 minutes. ☐ I realized what no longer serves me & imagined my problems healed. ☐ I made time for self-care today.

WEDNESDAY: _____/_____ **MOOD:** _____ **MOON PHASE** ◯

My "I am" Affirmation of the day: _____

Today I am grateful for: _____

I am manifesting: _____

☐ I visualized my dream coming true for 2-5 minutes. ☐ I realized what no longer serves me & imagined my problems healed. ☐ I made time for self-care today.

"If you don't like something change it; if you can't change it, change the way you think about it." —Mary Engelbreit

THURSDAY: _____ / _____   **MOOD:** _____   **MOON PHASE** ◯

My "I am" Affirmation of the day: _____

Today I am grateful for: _____

I am manifesting: _____

☐ I visualized my dream coming true for 2-5 minutes.   ☐ I realized what no longer serves me & imagined my problems healed.   ☐ I made time for self-care today.

FRIDAY: _____ / _____   **MOOD:** _____   **MOON PHASE** ◯

My "I am" Affirmation of the day: _____

Today I am grateful for: _____

I am manifesting: _____

☐ I visualized my dream coming true for 2-5 minutes.   ☐ I realized what no longer serves me & imagined my problems healed.   ☐ I made time for self-care today.

SATURDAY: _____ / _____   **MOOD:** _____   **MOON PHASE** ◯

My "I am" Affirmation of the day: _____

Today I am grateful for: _____

I am manifesting: _____

☐ I visualized my dream coming true for 2-5 minutes.   ☐ I realized what no longer serves me & imagined my problems healed.   ☐ I made time for self-care today.

SUNDAY: _____ / _____   **MOOD:** _____   **MOON PHASE** ◯

My "I am" Affirmation of the day: _____

Today I am grateful for: _____

I am manifesting: _____

☐ I visualized my dream coming true for 2-5 minutes.   ☐ I realized what no longer serves me & imagined my problems healed.   ☐ I made time for self-care today.

THE BEST THING THAT HAPPENED TO ME THIS WEEK WAS:

week 52

See the true beauty in yourself. Write what you appreciate about yourself—both your external appearance and your personality.

_____

_____

_____

MONDAY: ____ / ____   MOOD: _____   MOON PHASE ⚪

My "I am" Affirmation of the day: _____

Today I am grateful for: _____

I am manifesting: _____

☐ I visualized my dream coming true for 2–5 minutes.
☐ I realized what no longer serves me & imagined my problems healed.
☐ I made time for self-care today.

TUESDAY: ____ / ____   MOOD: _____   MOON PHASE ⚪

My "I am" Affirmation of the day: _____

Today I am grateful for: _____

I am manifesting: _____

☐ I visualized my dream coming true for 2–5 minutes.
☐ I realized what no longer serves me & imagined my problems healed.
☐ I made time for self-care today.

WEDNESDAY: ____ / ____   MOOD: _____   MOON PHASE ⚪

My "I am" Affirmation of the day: _____

Today I am grateful for: _____

I am manifesting: _____

☐ I visualized my dream coming true for 2–5 minutes.
☐ I realized what no longer serves me & imagined my problems healed.
☐ I made time for self-care today.

THURSDAY: _____ / _____   **MOOD:** _____   **MOON PHASE** ◯

My "I am" Affirmation of the day: _____

Today I am grateful for: _____

I am manifesting: _____

☐ I visualized my dream coming true for 2-5 minutes.   ☐ I realized what no longer serves me & imagined my problems healed.   ☐ I made time for self-care today.

FRIDAY: _____ / _____   **MOOD:** _____   **MOON PHASE** ◯

My "I am" Affirmation of the day: _____

Today I am grateful for: _____

I am manifesting: _____

☐ I visualized my dream coming true for 2-5 minutes.   ☐ I realized what no longer serves me & imagined my problems healed.   ☐ I made time for self-care today.

SATURDAY: _____ / _____   **MOOD:** _____   **MOON PHASE** ◯

My "I am" Affirmation of the day: _____

Today I am grateful for: _____

I am manifesting: _____

☐ I visualized my dream coming true for 2-5 minutes.   ☐ I realized what no longer serves me & imagined my problems healed.   ☐ I made time for self-care today.

SUNDAY: _____ / _____   **MOOD:** _____   **MOON PHASE** ◯

My "I am" Affirmation of the day: _____

Today I am grateful for: _____

I am manifesting: _____

☐ I visualized my dream coming true for 2-5 minutes.   ☐ I realized what no longer serves me & imagined my problems healed.   ☐ I made time for self-care today.

THE BEST THING THAT HAPPENED TO ME THIS WEEK WAS:

REFLECTIONS ON MY JOURNEY

You've done so much and have come so far, Beautiful Soul! Now, let's revisit a new version of our chart from our initial reflection. This will allow you to fully see and appreciate all the progress you've made, while providing you clarity on your vision moving forward. Write your reflections in each box below.

	Describe what you're currently experiencing in this area.
Career/School	
Finances	
Romantic relationships	
Relationships with friends and family	
Health and wellness	
Self-esteem and self-love	
Fun, travel, free time, hobbies	

How has this changed from your initial reflection?

	How do you now feel about this area of your life?
Career/School	
Finances	
Romantic relationships	
Relationships with friends and family	
Health and wellness	
Self-esteem and self-love	
Fun, travel, free time, hobbies	

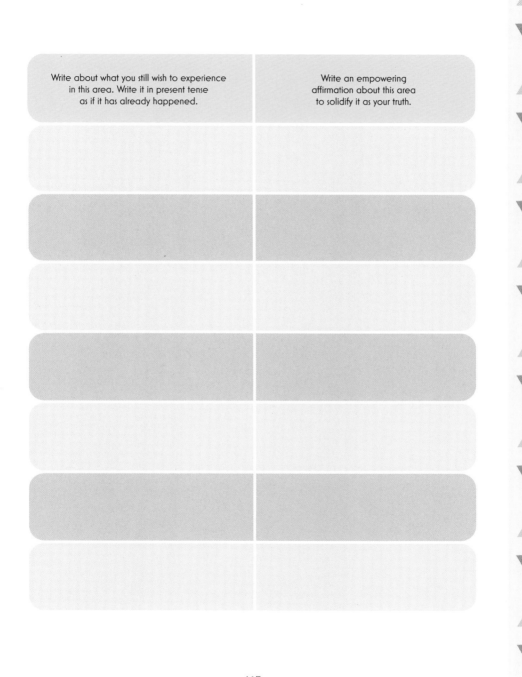

Write about what you still wish to experience in this area. Write it in present tense as if it has already happened.

Write an empowering affirmation about this area to solidify it as your truth.

What are you most proud of achieving this year?

How does your life feel differently? How has each area of your life improved?

How do you feel about yourself? Both inside and out?

How can you celebrate yourself? How will you honor your journey?

What were five moments that you loved this year?

What were the top five things you manifested and made happen this year?

Going forward, what kind of routine are you going to create to stay on track?

What goals do you still wish to achieve?

Write as if you've achieved these goals in present tense. Include how it would feel to achieve them.

In which ways will you commit to continuing this journey?

FINAL REFLECTIONS

conclusion

Be proud of yourself right now! I hope you know what a fantastic accomplishment completing this is. How amazing is it that you stuck to this workbook for a full year? Absolutely incredible! Do something to celebrate yourself. Eat cupcakes, buy yourself a gift, go out with your friends, buy some balloons, jump up and down, or have a personal dance party; whatever it is, celebrate yourself, and honor your journey. Show the universe how grateful you are that you did this. Because when we put out celebration energy, the universe will bring us more things to celebrate.

Remember, your success is inevitable because you were sent here to succeed. You wouldn't be given a desire if it wasn't meant for you to make it happen. The fact that you can imagine it, means you can do it!

You've got this, Beautiful Soul. I'm sending you so much love and wishing you all the best going forward. You are an amazing, magical being and you absolutely can make your dreams come true. As you move forward with this journey, continue to dedicate yourself to these practices. Your transformation this past year is proof that sticking to daily exercises can really go a long way and make a huge difference. Keep choosing to see the magic in your everyday life and always remember to find joy in the journey.

Resources

I am beyond grateful for all the amazing minds who have shared their wisdom and contributed to the cultivation of my own mindset practices. I've been a student of personal development for over a decade and have learned so much from so many amazing teachers. Personal development is a lifelong practice, so to keep your studies going. Here are my recommendations for some amazing resources:

BOOKS

Super Attractor: Methods for Manifesting a Life beyond Your Wildest Dreams, Gabrielle Bernstein

Ask and it is Given: Learning to Manifest Your Desires Esther and Jerry Hicks

Think Like a Monk: Train Your Mind for Peace and Purpose Every Day Jay Shetty

You Are a Badass at Making Money: Master the Mindset of Wealth Jen Sincero

Manifest Now, Idil Ahmed

Good Vibes, Good Life: How Self-Love Is the Key to Unlocking Your Greatness, Vex King

Make it Happen: Manifest the Life of Your Dreams Jordanna Levin

It's Your Universe, Ashley Eckstein

ABOUT THE AUTHOR

Erica Rose is an author, artist, and spiritual mentor from Long Island, New York. A lifelong writer and artist, Erica has a BFA from the School of Visual Arts. She started pursuing studies in the spiritual world as a teenager, after a friend's psychic grandma taught her that anyone can be psychic, it's just a matter of developing your natural intuition. Erica has since become a mindset master through studying all aspects of card reading, channeling spirits, meditation, and manifestation. With over a decade of spiritual knowledge, Erica started her inspirational Instagram account in 2018, attracting quite a following from sharing bright, colorful, empowering messages infused with magic. Erica's mission is to help everyone believe in themselves and believe that all of their dreams can come true. You can follow Erica on Instagram at @LaRoseDesReves

Inspiring | Educating | Creating | Entertaining

Brimming with creative inspiration, how-to
projects, and useful information to enrich your
everyday life, quarto.com is a favorite destination
for those pursuing their interests and passions.

This edition published in 2022 by Chartwell Books,
an imprint of The Quarto Group
142 West 36th Street, 4th Floor
New York, NY 10018 USA
T (212) 779-4972 F (212) 779-6058
www.Quarto.com

Contains content originally published as *Finding Joy in the Journey Journal*
in 2022 by Rock Point, an imprint of The Quarto Group,
142 West 36th Street, 4th Floor, New York, NY 10018, USA
T (212) 779-4972 F (212) 779-6058 www.Quarto.com

10 9 8 7 6 5 4 3 2 1

Chartwell titles are also available at discount for retail, wholesale, promotional,
and bulk purchase. For details, contact the Special Sales Manager by email at
specialsales@quarto.com or by mail at The Quarto Group, Attn: Special Sales
Manager, 100 Cummings Center Suite 265D, Beverly, MA 01915, USA.

ISBN: 978-0-7858-4123-4

Publisher: Rage Kindelsperger
Creative Director: Laura Drew
Managing Editor: Cara Donaldson
Editor: Sara Bonacum
Interior Design: Kim Winscher

Printed in China

*This workbook provides general information that tends to evoke feelings of strength
and confidence. However, it should not be relied upon as recommending or promoting
any specific diagnosis or method of treatment for a particular condition, and it is not
intended as a substitute for medical advice or for direct diagnosis and treatment of a
medical condition by a qualified physician. Readers who have questions about a particular
condition, possible treatments for that condition, or possible reactions from the condition
or its treatment should consult a physician or other qualified healthcare professional.*